THE FINANCIAL
ADVISOR
TO BUILDING
WEALTH

PURSUING PROSPERITY
WITH FINANCIAL EDUCATION

Thomas Herold - Fall 2011 Edition

The Financial Advisor to Building Wealth

Pursuing Prosperity
with Financial Education

Fall 2011 Edition

Revision 1.1

Thomas Herold
Dream Manifesto, LLC.
© 2005-2011 All rights reserved.

www.wealthbuildingcourse.com

Table of Contents

<u>INTRODUCTION</u>

"Pursuing Prosperity with Financial Education"

Introduction

Welcome to the Financial Advisor to Building Your Wealth

It's my pleasure to present the fall 2011 edition of our quarterly publication 'Financial Advisor to Building Wealth'.

Just take a moment and think about what wealth means to you. If you're like most folk, you think it's all about money. It was for me too, until I decided to explore the topic more deeply and really consider what makes us wealthy, prosperous people. Wealth, for me, is not merely material possessions: it's your health, your life-style and relationships, even your mental abilities.

Curious yet? If you still think money has anything to do with wealth, you'll be in for a big surprise when you read this issue. My main aim, and the inspiration for my website and the whole of my work, is to help you learn about finance like I did – to help you transform your life, leave the past behind and take control of your wealth. Now, you might think financial terminology is about as interesting as a bag of rice falling off a shelf in China. But these days, one of the most essential and precious gifts you can give yourself is a financial education - especially given the worldwide economic crisis we are all experiencing.

Humanity is embarking on the biggest transfer of wealth in history. You may have sensed it already, and you're right: wealth is flowing at breathtaking speeds away from the financially uneducated to-wards people who know about finance and, crucially, how to use that knowledge to their advantage.

The current international financial crisis is a direct outcome of government and bank interventions. It's time for us to open our eyes to this and start to protect ourselves.

You might have heard the phrase, "If you always do what you've always done, you'll always get what you've always got." There's no question that, in order to secure your future and live a life that you're in control of, you must take on the task of understanding what is happening to your hard-earned money.

Once you grasp and unravel the hidden agenda of a few powerful people, you will be able to choose and reclaim your financial freedom. At the moment, this may all sound like a conspiracy theory to you; however, the research and facts contained in this book will provide you with enough evidence that there is a plan behind all this, which right now is serving other people, not you.

You'll realize that this plan is nothing new, and that the past shows similar attempts at monetary control and failure. Learning about these will make you better able to react to the present, and start creating wealth for yourself, rather than other people.

I've structured the articles into several categories. Feel free to skip between them and simply read what interests you most. Remember: this is not a course that you're doing for anyone else. This is a gift to yourself. Read the articles that apply to you, and in doing so you will broaden your knowledge and feel more qualified to keep learning and growing your wealth.

All the articles have been taken from the Wealth Building Course website and assembled here for you to make your financial learning simpler and more convenient. I've left out several articles which focused on issues that have now been overtaken by events. The situation is constantly changing, but the articles here have been carefully selected for their continuing relevance.

Enjoy your reading and always keep learning. Allow your mind to open up to new ideas. Believe that you can change your approach to wealth, and transform your life. As Steve Jobs once said: "Stay hungry, stay foolish."

Thomas Herold

Investing

Investing

<u>INVESTING</u>

"Putting Energy to Work"

Investing

What Country Is the Safest Place to Invest Your Money?

In these days when even some Western developed economies are considered to be unsafe places to invest, you may wonder which ones are good locations for you to invest your money. In the past, this information was often a matter of speculation or a financial adviser's opinion.

Now, there is a well respected indicator that tells you the five safest and least safest countries for your money. In the following paragraphs, you will learn what the Index of Sovereign Risk is, what countries are the safest places for your money, what are the most dangerous ones in which to invest, and where the U.S. ranks in the list and why.

What is the Index of Sovereign Risk?

The indicator that ranks the nations of the world according to the risk of their government debt is called the Index of Sovereign Risk. BlackRock, the biggest publicly traded manager of assets, created this measurement in response to the bigger economic macro themes of the U.S. debt ceiling and the European debt crisis. These types of macro investments have received a greater amount of cash inflow this year than any of the other hedge fund categories.

This index is crafted more precisely than factors that other money managers consider. The typical method of discovering which country has the safest bonds is done through analysis of a nation's debt as compared to its gross domestic product, or total of all goods and services produced there in a year. The BlackRock index includes an extensive variety of other factors. These are grouped by four overall categories of external finance position, how close they are to distress, their willingness to pay the debts, and the health of their banking sector.

Which Country is the Safest Place to Invest In and Why?

You may be surprised to learn that the least risky country in the world to invest in is Norway. According to BlackRock, there are a number of reasons why their bonds are considered to be rock solid. Norway has very low risks of experiencing an internal or external financial system shock. Their financial institutions are strong. Perhaps most importantly, their total amounts of debt are incredibly low.

Norway also enjoys a number of very positive attributes. They practice conservative fiscal policies. They benefit from a large amount of energy resources in their share of North Sea Oil that amounts to around three hundred thousand dollars in proven oil reserves for every resident. This is evidenced as they remain the ninth largest exporter of oil on earth. As the country with the seventh largest GDP per person, they export machinery, chemicals, metals, ships, and fish, beyond oil.

It is true that no country is without faults. Norway is said to be somewhat dependent on the price of oil.

But even if this is true to a point, BlackRock points out that the credit of Norway easily embodies the lowest odds of devaluation, default, or above normal inflation rates. How many other countries today can say the same?

Why Is It Difficult to Invest in Norway's Bonds?

The downside to Norway's excellent low levels of debt is that there are not so many Norwegian bonds for you and other careful investors to buy. You could purchase the Global X FTSE Norway 30 Exchange Traded Fund instead. Keep in mind that the best credit countries are not always those with the best performance stocks.

What Are the Other Safest Countries to Invest In?

There are four other highly ranked safe countries in the top five of the Index of Sovereign Risk whose government bonds you might consider. Sweden, Switzerland, Finland, and Australia rank as the next four best places after Norway. All of these nations have low debt, stable banks, and diversified economies that support their governments and financial outlooks.

What Are the Least Safe Countries In Which to Invest Your Money?

If you contemplate other countries in which to invest your money, there are some that you should stay away from especially. The Index of Sovereign Risk ranks the five most dangerous places to buy government bonds as well.

It is no surprise that Greece is the least safe country with its enormous bailouts that have grabbed headlines around the globe. Close behind it are Portugal with its bailout needs and high debt load, Venezuela with its dictator Chavez who is not afraid to default on debt or nationalize companies and investments, Egypt with an uncertain political future under its martial rule, and Italy that is also heavily loaded down with debt and a less competitive economy.

Where Does the U.S. Debt Rank As a Safe Place for Your Money?

The U.S. has long been considered to be among the safest places to keep your money by individuals and investors. This status as ultimate safe haven has been challenged in the last few years since the financial crisis and Great Recession.

The Index of Sovereign Risk places the U.S. at the number fifteen safest country to keep your money, behind Canada at number six and China at number fourteen, while still ahead of the United Kingdom at twenty two. The reasons that the U.S. received a relatively low rank as compared to fourteen other countries can be explained by a recent statement of the non-partisan Congressional Budget Office, or CBO, where they said that the U.S. is rapidly heading towards the most predictable financial crisis in its history.

Is the U.S. Headed for European-Style Debt Crisis?

The CBO has released a lengthy report that helps to explain why the U.S. is ranked at fifteen for safest countries in which to buy bonds. This official government agency bears the responsibility to determine the economic outcomes of government legislation and policy.

They explain that the country's debt burden that is swiftly growing has boosted the odds that there will be a serious U.S. financial crisis as investors' confidence in U.S. bonds deteriorates. This would force the American government to enact harsh and draconian cuts in spending or to massively increase taxes in order to avoid default on its debt. It would also mean that the U.S. fell off of the credit cliff and was no longer able to borrow from credit markets at affordable interest rates.

The rank of fifteenth safest place to park your money is similarly influence by predictions from the CBO. They say that because the government borrows in excess of forty cents of each dollar that it spends, the national debt is going to rise dramatically in the near future. They project that it will reach one hundred nine percent of national GDP before or by 2023.

The last reason that the CBO gives you for why the U.S. is ranked relatively low for safe places to buy bonds lies in the possibility of a sudden fiscal crisis. They warn you that investors could lose confidence overnight in the American government's capability to manage its finances competently. If this were to occur, the investors who tripped over each other on their way to the U.S. government debt exit doors would demand double digit interest rates to hold U.S. debt. This would instantly make the unsustainable financial position of the U.S. government far worse.

Is it any wonder that the U.S. ranks lower than China now for safe countries in which to invest your money?

Huge Positive Momentum Is Coming To Gold And Silver

As you look for reasons to buy gold and silver today, there is yet another new one that you may not have considered before now. This lies in the fact that the Chinese are launching their own Pan Asian Precious Metals Exchange this very month of July.

Andrew Maguire has been among the first to report on this exciting story. In the following paragraphs, you will learn about the huge impact that this new Chinese metals exchange is set to have on available supply, demand, and the price for both gold and silver in the months that come.

Who Is Andrew Maguire?

Andrew Maguire is a former Goldman Sachs metals trader. He has more than forty years of experience in this arena and has broken other major precious metals stories in the past. Last year, he gave an exclusive interview of his notification to the CFTC, or Commodity Futures Trading Commission, that fraud and price manipulation were being committed in both the silver and gold markets.

This fraud that he alleged concerns banks, nations, and leaders of countries. It could turn out to be the biggest example of fraud in the history of the world. His latest news about the new gold and silver market that will open in July 2011 in China gives him reason to call for silver prices of over a hundred dollars per ounce.

What Is the New Pan Asia Precious Metals Exchange that China Will Open?

China will begin to offer a new gold and silver mini contract in July on their new Pan Asian Gold Exchange. By itself this is huge news, as it establishes a new center for gold and silver that will offer a third daily settlement for these precious metals' prices besides those of London and Chicago.

The biggest news is that these metals will trade valued in the Chinese currency the RMB, or remnibi. In fact, this Pan Asia Gold Exchange is solidly backed by both the Chinese security regulatory commission as well as the state administration for foreign exchange.

The most obvious effect of this new exchange is that it is forecast to provide enormous ongoing additional demand to bolster gold and silver prices. Besides this, it is a clear attempt of the Chinese government to usher the remnibi rapidly on to the major international currency stage. Gold and silver are likely to experience major shock waves this summer as these effects reverberate throughout the precious metals markets.

How Will This Affect The Demand and Price of Silver and Gold?

While silver currently trades in the mid $30's per ounce range, you may wonder how respected analysts like Andrew Maguire can predict silver at three times its present day price. You have to realize how tight the available gold and especially silver supplies are in order to understand how this is possible. To know this, consider how many Chinese will be tied in to this new precious metals exchange.

This will be the first time that the Chinese people and businesses have possessed the opportunity to acquire gold and silver without physically purchasing it. The first contract that the exchange will offer is a ten ounce gold mini contract. It goes live in July.

The Agricultural Bank of China is tied directly in to this exchange, with its three hundred and twenty million customers. If only one percent of their customers purchased a single mini contract, then the exchange would have to obtain and warehouse a thousand tons of gold in order to cover these contracts. This would exhaust most of the available gold stocks that exist above ground.

The Pan Asian Gold Exchange silver contract is a five hundred ounce silver mini contract. The effect of a one percent purchase by the Agricultural Bank of China's three hundred twenty million customers would require 1.6 billion ounces of physical silver to be found. The silver supply situation is even tighter than the gold market.

There are not even a hundred million ounces of silver available above ground, much less sixteen times as many. The silver needs simply could not be filled at any price. The likely result on the world silver markets would be a major price gap higher to fifty or a hundred dollars per ounce on one or more open days. All of the investors who are short silver would be forced into a technical default and would probably have to settle their contracts for cash as soon as they could.

Silver prices are totally different from gold. The prices of silver have been artificially held down by banks and companies who sold them short illegally for years. The price of silver that you have witnessed for decades now has been a virtual price. This price has not accurately reflected the incredibly tight supply and demand situation.

One thing that the new Chinese Pan Asian exchange will do is to help rectify this false imbalance in the silver prices. Some analysts estimate that real silver prices may be recognized as high as from $300 to $500 per ounce in time.

How Will This Affect the Chinese Currency Holdings?

The other major effect that this new exchange will create relates to the Chinese massive dollar currency reserves and the value of the dollar. Today, the Chinese look at their dollar holdings as if they are a sand that runs through their fingers.

They wish to get out of them as fast as they can. Because of this mindset towards U.S. dollars, the Chinese urgently look for anything of tangible value that they can buy. This includes forests, mines, oil reserves, businesses, real estate, highest quality rare art and objects, and precious metals.

In the past, they have purchased GLD and SLV Exchange Traded Funds and cashed these out for physical gold and silver holdings. Now with their Pan Asian Gold Exchange, they will be able to more rapidly sell additional holdings of their three trillion U.S. dollars to buy gold and silver that are valued in their own currency. The ramifications for the future value of the U.S. dollar are grim.

Investors will also no longer be forced to purchase gold in only U.S. Dollars, Pounds, Euros, and Swiss Francs. Now international investors will be given the chance and the choice to buy gold in Chinese Yuan. You can believe that a significant part of future gold purchases from Asia will go through this Chinese exchange.

Beyond this, Andrew Maguire theorizes that much of the world precious metals business will be attracted to these gold and silver contracts on their new exchange, as it will offer another alternative where they are able to purchase and sell contracts for physical silver and gold. The value of the Chinese currency will rise as a direct result of this new demand that funnels into precious metals.

Gold and silver themselves will also see a new time of the day where they fluctuate substantially in price because of the new Pan Asian Gold Exchange. This will occur every day at the new price fixing that will be established at the Beijing 8 AM time.

Huge positive momentum is coming to gold and silver. Can you think of a better time to establish positions in these two precious metals than now?

Gold And Silver Investment Advice From Theodore Butler

Gold and silver investments have become all the rage in the last few years. With the continuing uncertainty that you see in geopolitical events, runaway governments' spending, and effects of the Great Recession and financial collapse that still reverberate through the world economy, the precious metals are once again a necessary component of everyone's diversified investment portfolio.

For anyone who is a novice investor in gold or silver, you are going to need some reliable and solid information to help you get started with your purchase decisions. You will find that there is much more to gold and silver investing than simply giving the order to buy. One website that offers a huge amount of information and resources, as well as a place to purchase your gold and silver, is Investment Rarities Incorporated.

What is Investment Rarities Incorporated?

Investment Rarities Incorporated, also known by its initials IRI, is a gold and silver dealer that has been actively engaged in the business for more than thirty five years. The company is one of the more established outfits in the precious metals business today. They have delivered in excess of two billion dollars in both silver and gold bullion and coins to their clients over the years.

What makes them different from some outfits out there is that they stick with the principal of tangible delivery of products. This means that they do not allow you to own precious metals through the use of leverage. When you buy coins or bullion from them, the coins arrive at your door and you own them personally.

Who Are the Main Principals of Investment Rarities Incorporated?

Jim Cook is the founder and President of IRI. He prides himself as a gold coin business pioneer from the 1970's. Jim started out as a coin collector in the 1970's and built this into a significant business that is among the leaders in the precious metals sales and information fields today. The Minneapolis based enterprise that he started incorporates thirty different companies now.

Ted Butler is the premier writer of IRI's newsletter and website content. He has been in the precious metals business for over thirty five years. His fans call him quite possibly the most knowledgeable individual on earth where the world silver market is concerned.

This long time silver icon can claim to be the first analyst who publicly acknowledged and opined on the scandal in the currently under investigation silver market manipulation that concerns the lending and illegal short selling of silver. His work on this subject was literally years ahead of the competition.

Ted can be called the one man most responsible for making the regulatory authorities recognize and investigate the problems regarding this so called deceptive leasing of precious metals. As a long time newsletter writer, he has over ten years of experience writing the Gloom and Doom newsletter for IRI. Ted now publishes his own subscription based newsletter under his Butler Research as well.

What Does Investment Rarities Incorporated Offer You on their Website?

IRI boasts an almost embarrassing collection of material that is offered at no charge to you as an interested prospect in precious metals investments, a customer, or merely someone who wants to know more about why silver and gold are so important these days.

There are two sections of great quotes both past and present, a special reports section, an archived Gloom and Doom newsletters section, links to other well known third party financial and precious metals newsletters, a recommended model portfolios in gold and silver section, and gold and silver coin and bullion descriptions sections.

You should look through all of the various sections as they offer everyone from the novice to the advanced precious metals investor or prospect an enormous amount of free informational resources that can take your investment financial education to a whole new level.

What is In the Special Reports Section?

There are a wealth of special reports included at no charge on this website. You will be amazed at all of the topics that you can find really good, accurate information on where precious metals are concerned. Topics include a basic primer to Silver and gold, silver as the miracle metal, biggest factors in future silver prices, silver IRA's, silver products, and an upcoming industrial panic for silver.

Inside the Gloom and Doom Newsletter and IRI Blog Sections

If you are interested in receiving free copes of the Gloom and doom Newsletter that James Cook and Ted Butler produce twice every month, you can call them on their toll free number or email them. As a potential prospect, they will send you the current newsletters for ten months, and as a customer, you will get them for three years from your last purchase.

The archives section has older copies of the newsletter available to you for free download. There is also a new IRI blog section where they discuss things of interest in the gold and silver metals markets.

What Other Newsletters Are Sourced on the Site?

There are the best of a number of widely followed economics and precious metals newsletter writers available to you on the site. Of course you can see Ted Butler's commentaries and Jim Cook's current thoughts.

Besides this, you will find articles on and interviews with twenty-four different experts. Among these are ShadowStats writer John Williams, metals expert Peter Schiff, and long time newsletter icon Howard Ruff.

What is the Portfolios Breakdown Section About?

IRI outlines a model portfolio allocation for you as a new gold and silver investor. For gold, they offer sample portfolios for what you should buy with $10,000, $50,000, and $100,000 sized portfolios. For silver, they give ideal portfolio breakdowns for $10,000, $25,000, $50,000, and $100,000.

For example, IRI suggests that if you have $10,000 to spend on gold holdings, that you acquire $5,000 in one ounce Vienna Philharmonics, the most popular gold coin made in Europe, and $5,000 in U.S. Twenty Dollar Gold pieces that are of the Saint-Gaudens variety.

If you have $10,000 to invest in silver, they recommend that you purchase a combination of U.S. Silver Eagles coins and other ninety percent silver coins, such as pre-1965 dimes, quarters, half dollars, and silver dollars.

What Can You Learn in the Coins Description Sections?

The website has a particularly interesting section on gold coins, and they also offer descriptions of various silver products under its own heading. For example, did you know that Twenty Dollar Gold Pieces of St. Gaudens' variety are considered to be the most beautiful coin in the world as well as being the most popular gold coin that America makes?

You probably also do not know that the South African Krugerrand is the most common gold coin on earth, since more of these have been produced by far than any other national type. You will find the Buffalo Gold Coins interesting as well, since they are twenty-four karat gold coins at the purity rate of 99.99%.

You will also discover here the different denominations that these coins are sold in, like half ounce, quarter ounce, and even tenth ounce of gold sizes in the Austrian Vienna Philharmonic.

The Investment Rarities Incorporated may be a for profit business that sells gold and silver bullion, coins, and even silverware flat-ware, but they are serious about educated customers and prospects too. Where else can you find this much free financial education and information in one site on the Internet?

You can find Investment Rarities Incorporated at:
www.investmentrarities.com

Why The Toughest Investment Lesson Is Doing Nothing

You have always been warned about get rich quick schemes, even though you may never have understood why. What is possibly wrong with becoming wealthy overnight? The answer is that in order for you to build up lasting wealth effectively, you must employ a long term strategy.

The great Confederate General Robert E. Lee had some very appropriate quotes on the subject of patience. When he was asked about how he decided on his military command appointments, he said that he could not place in command of other people an individual who was unable to control himself.

This is why the hardest lesson that you can learn where your investments are concerned is the lesson to be patient. In the paragraphs below, you will understand why doing nothing is often the most effective way to improve your investment performance over the long term time frame.

Why is the Simplest Lesson of Sound Investing Also the Most Difficult?

The simplest lesson for you to learn and utilize in your own investments is one of patience. In theory, this is so easy and obvious that you could even train a monkey to do it.

While it sounds too basic to simply do nothing where your investments are concerned, the actual practice of this often proves to be extraordinarily difficult for the majority of people. Consider how few individuals are able to accomplish the art of waiting and doing nothing.

The reason that doing nothing is so critically important for your investment strategy is because the major gains that you will make in your investment career lie in the few really big trades. The nature of these necessary big trades is such that they do not appear on a daily, weekly, or monthly basis. In fact, just the opposite is true.

The really big trades are rare and wonderful.

For you to successfully make much money in your life, you will have to find the really big trades, which can be the easy part. Then you must discipline yourself effectively so that you can wait out the successful gems of trades. It is not so hard to find a winning trade.

It is extremely hard to allow such a trade both the time and opportunity to run, in order for it to reach the really big returns. If you are unable to learn this simple to grasp yet hard to practice skill, then you will never become truly wealthy through investments.

Legendary Investor Jesse Livermore Teaches Patience in Investing

In 1923, a legendary investor Jesse Livermore published a book called "Reminiscences of a Stock Operator." In this book, he summed up the importance of doing nothing in your investment strategy.

He stated that he had been involved with Wall Street for a number of years. In this amount of time, he had both made and lost millions of dollars.

Jesse tells you that his thinking and plotting never made him really big money. Instead, it was when he sat and waited that he captured the big returns. Individuals who are able to be right and patient are rare and unusual indeed. It may surprise you to learn that the patient part is the more elusive quality of the two.

Recent Examples of Huge Trades That Required Doing Nothing

At the end of 2006, the housing market sent signals that it was going to crash and burn. Shrewd investors like Goldman Sachs Bank and hedge fund manager Henry Paulson realized this and took positions against the housing market. Others shorted stocks and waited for the inevitable crash. The markets plummeted more than fifty percent over the next three years. To capture the really big gains and not simply bank ten to twenty percent, you had to wait almost three long and tumultuous years.

In March of 2009, the stock market finally reached a bottom in the wake of the devastating financial crisis that began in 2007. If you were among the individuals who realized this at the time, you might have purchased stocks aggressively. You could have made fifty percent if you had bought in and then held on tightly by doing nothing until 2011. To realize these fantastic gains, it required that you took no action for two exuberant years though.

Back in 2001/2002, gold had bottomed out at $250 per ounce. Many pundits were calling for the end of gold as a serious commodity. They simply scoffed at the archaic notion of gold as a currency. Even wealthy G7 nation Great Britain chose to dump half of its once considerable gold reserves at this pitiful low price point. If you bought in at that shockingly low price of $250 to $300 per ounce, then you could have doubled your money by 2006.

In order to realize the more considerable gains of five hundred percent, you would have to sit tight for another five years. Some analysts, such as Standard Chartered Bank of London, would tell you that selling at today's prices of over $1,600 per ounce is too soon. There may be prices as high as $5,000 plus per ounce of gold in the future for those of you with the patience to sit still on your gold holdings and do nothing.

Silver is another case in point. At the beginning of this new millennium, you could acquire silver for a song price of $4.50 per ounce. It could hardly be mined from the earth at this cost. You who possessed some foresight and patience purchased this other precious metal and waited for eight years. In 2009, you might have sold it for a tidy four hundred percent profit at $18 per ounce.

Those of you who exercised patience a little longer and did nothing might have realized upwards of $50 per ounce, or a thousand percent return, in 2010. Once again, the best is still yet to come for silver, so even if you took profits at $50 an ounce, you might be cheating yourself of the opportunity to make some really serious gains in the ongoing silver bull market.

The greatest opportunities may yet lie ahead for you if you can but learn the critical lesson to sit and do nothing. We live in the middle of the famous Big Ben Bernake Asset Bubble.

By the time that the Federal Reserve has finished devaluing the U.S. dollar with cheap interest rates and their electronic printing presses that are working around the clock, this might end up being the most spectacular asset bubble that the world has ever witnessed in gold, silver, and stocks. To emerge a winner from it though, you will have to place your proverbial bets wisely, then walk away while they grow, grow, grow.

Impatience is your most powerful and constantly lurking arch enemy. Do not give up your screaming winner investments too hastily or easily. You should not settle for a paltry doubling of your money when you can instead realize gains of possibly multiple thousands of percent simply by waiting. You might emerge from the present economic turbulence far wealthier than you can possibly imagine.

Ask yourself a deep question - how often do these kinds of enormous opportunities present themselves in one life time?

The 12 Investment Myths And The Quest to Create Wealth

In the scary stock markets of today, you may find yourself in need of financial education that can help you to avoid investment mistakes. Fortunately, there is a book on the market that offers you just this type of advice.

"The 12 Investing Myths: Why Individual Investors Are Failing Miserably and How You Can Avoid Being One of Them" reveals the myths of investing that will hold you back from the kinds of gains that you need to realize in your quest to create wealth.

Who is the Author Jack Calhoun?

Jack Calhoun serves as the Capital Directions, LLC managing principal. This firm is among the biggest of the Atlanta area investment advisory companies. His extensive writings on the basics of successful investment include credits in Investors' Business Daily, The Wall Street Journal, and the Atlanta Journal-Constitution. Besides his role with Capital Directions and his writing, he also speaks professionally to investment clubs and professional associations on topics that are related to investments.

What is the Premise of The 12 Investing Myths?

Over the long term, the stock market has created enormous wealth for investors like you. The problem is that the majority of investors never become rich through their investments in the stock market. Quite the opposite is true for most investors.

You may be among the majority who boast sad stock market stories that range from a total disaster to simply insufficient returns to reach your goals. "The 12 Investment Myths" explores the topic of why there is a disconnect between the money that some few people make in the stock market and the money that you actually make in the stock market.

The answer to this disparity of stock market success lies in a group of beliefs that you may hold along with the majority of people who own stocks. These myths appear to be solidly based when you look at them casually. The sad truth is that they are the templates for stock market failure. Where do these myths originate?

On Wall Street, which is able to make enormous amounts of money because of this emotionally driven investment mentality. The financial media is also to blame in the spread of these myths. They desperately need material to fill their networks, and when they encourage these ideas that most investors thrive on, they garner the ratings that they need. Unfortunately, the victim of these 12 myths is you and the overwhelming majority of stock traders and investors.

What Are the 12 Myths that the Book Discusses?

Every chapter in "The 12 Investment Myths" pertains to one of the false ideas that far too many investors hold dear. These chapters consider the issue that is a part of the myth in detail.

Then they provide you with another answer to how you can side step this pitfall. The first myth is that a smart investor ought to be able to outperform the market. While this is true for a very few investors, it is really difficult for the vast majority.

Myth number two says that Brokerage firms are set up to service their clients. This could not be farther from the truth. Brokerage firms exist to trade their own money. Besides this, they want to make commissions on your trades.

The third myth claims that performance is all that matters. While this is true to a point, there are other things to consider in your investments, such as how will the stock do over the longer term. A stock might be undervalued, even if the management of the company is not doing everything right.

Myth four says that activity is good. When you trade stocks too much, the only person that it is good for is your broker, who makes a commission with every trade. You also can lose on the difference between what you pay for an investment and the price at which the market will buy it back from you. Over time and many trades, this adds up to huge amounts of money.

The fifth myth states that investors make a decent living. This is true for some investors, some of the time. Many investors make and lose whole fortunes in one life time. The majority of people who trade stocks do it emotionally and lose or just come out a little bit ahead.

Myth number six tells you that the media is a terrific place to get your investment advice. The talking heads on CNBC, Bloomberg, and the Fox Business network exist for one reason.

This is to provide entertainment that generates good ratings, so that advertisers will pay generously for commercials during the break. They do not have your best interest at heart.

The seventh myth states that you should put your money into companies that are good. The problem is that companies that are good are already fairly valued most of the time. The ones that gain most significantly in value are often ones that are unknown or up and coming. You had never heard of Apple once upon a time, but it made you incredibly rich if you knew to buy it before it became a "good" company.

Myth number eight claims that investing is actually exciting. It is not so exciting for the people who put in hours of research, and patiently wait for the right trade to come along. It is nerve wracking for day traders, who often lose everything or never make a living at it.

The ninth myth states that risk is always the same. Risk is never the same, and it can actually be quantified. You can also take measures to reduce risk with investments.

A popular tenth myth is that the end of the world is upon us, so there is no point to invest. No one knows for certain if the markets will crash and burn this year, or in 2012 for that matter. If you bury your head in the sand, then you will not make any money in the meanwhile. In ten years from now with this attitude, you can be certain that your money will not have grown enough to support your retirement or other financial goals.

The eleventh myth is that you are not a market timer. Timing the markets is difficult, but not impossible. You can learn to time it to a point with enough financial education.

The final myth states that investment advisers' role is to make opportunities for you. Their job is actually to make sales and commissions. They are not going to spend their days looking for extra ways to make you money. No one cares about your money more than you do.

What Are the Four Principles of Investment Success?

Jack Calhoun also gives you the four principles of investment success in this book. He tells you that you must diversify your money across a number of different stocks and types of assets. You have to take control of your costs of investment and taxes so that you do not pay too much. The hardest lessons to learn and apply are to be patient and to control your emotions. If you can learn to apply these last two principles, then you will be years ahead of the typical investor.

What is the Final Verdict of the 12 Investing Myths?

Many finance books are written in a dense style that is hard to follow. Others require that you have serious financial training or an economics degree to understand them. This is not the case with "The 12 Investment Myths." Jack Calhoun wrote it so that any beginner can understand it.

His principles of investment are easy to grasp, and they make a very strong case for why you continue to struggle with investments. The bonus is that the book contains interesting stories, and the author demonstrates a good sense of humor.

Will you continue to make the same mistakes over and over again like everyone else, or will you educate yourself to be the one in the crowd who actually grows wealthy from investments?

The Shocking Truth of Wall Streets Investment Performance

When you look back on the performance of your investment portfolio over the last ten years, it might make you want to cry.

You are probably like most people who do not see returns that inspire when you consider the time frame that began the week before the 9/11/01 terrorist attacks and extends through the financial crisis that still roils the markets the first week of August 2011.

It might make you feel better about your own probably disappointing past investment decade when you compare it to the overall Wall Street indexes, mutual funds, and even some well known blue chip stocks.

In the paragraphs below, you will learn what the real and shocking truth is about Wall Street's investment performance from September 1, 2001 to the first week of August 2011. Be forewarned; the results are not pretty, especially when you measure them against inflation adjusted dollars over this time period.

A Moment of Truth: How Have the S&P 500, Dow Jones, and Nasdaq Indexes Performed Over the Last Ten Years?

Your broker will quickly tell you with great conviction that stocks are always the place to park your money over the long term.

He throws around numbers that sound impressive and seem too good to be true. This is because they are not true.

Consider the long term time frame of the last ten years.

The S&P 500 is perhaps the broadest, and almost universally recognized measurement for U.S. stocks. In the first week of September 2001, it opened at 1133. As of the first few days of August, it is at 1246. This represents a not too impressive change of plus 9% in ten years. So the S&P 500 basket of five hundred large and well known American corporations is up not even one percent per year in the last decade.

Another popular measurement of major stocks is the Dow Jones Industrial Average that represents the thirty so called blue chip companies of America. This index sat at 9,947 on the open of September 1, 2001. The first week of August 2011 saw it reach 12,144. It has outperformed the broader S&P 500 by a margin of two to one. This amounts to a whopping 18.1% over ten years, or 1.8% average return each year.

If you had instead parked your investment dollars in the technology heavy weight NASDAQ stock market index, then you would have fared better by far. Back in 2001, the NASDAQ languished at the end of the dot com bust. The level on September 1, 2001 stood at 1,802. August 3, 2011 witnessed a NASDAQ market level of 2,791.

This fairly impressive index has risen by 55% in the past decade. If you had the foresight to believe in technology in those days, you would have gained 5.5% a year.

This is far better than the S&P 500 and DJIA 30, but is still a far cry away from the phenomenal returns that your stock broker touts for stocks over the much vaunted "long term."

How Have Major Mutual Funds Performed During the LastTen Years?

"Fine," your stock broker might respond when you remind him about the lackluster performance of the past ten years in the major indexes. "But professional money managers have outdone these results," he will argue. Mutual funds are professionally managed vehicles that acquire many different stocks, bonds, and sometimes other types of investments.

Have they really done better than the major indexes over ten years? The answer depends on which mutual funds you discuss. There are thousands of mutual funds out there from which you can pick. The problem is that you never know which mutual funds are going to outperform the major averages.

The mutual funds are quick to point out in their prospectus that past performance is no guarantee of future returns. Mutual funds that perform the best one year fall out of favor and performance the next. The star of 2001 might have been a dog ten years later.

As a case in point, look at two popular funds run by one of the largest and most popular mutual fund families over the past decade and more, Fidelity Funds. Ten years ago, financial stocks were the darling of Wall Street and led in innovation and profits.

Fidelity Select Financial Services Portfolio, with a symbol of FIDSX, was a popular choice. On 9/1/01 the mutual fund opened at $102.04.

By 8/3/11 in the wake of the financial crisis that destroyed the banking industry, it stood at a mere $54.44. In ten years time, this darling of the financial industry is down 46.6%, or minus 4.66% each year on average.

If you had been more fortunate, you might have chosen the health care sector instead of the financial industry. The Fidelity Select Medical Delivery Fund purchased stocks in the health care business. It returned an average of 12.8% in the past ten years.

In general, mutual funds have followed the performance of either the broader market averages or the fortunes of the specific industry that they tracked. Some have been better than others, but practically none of them have delivered the amazing results that your broker touts whenever you talk with him.

How Have Major Blue Chip Stocks Performed During the Last Ten Years?

If your broker points out that some individual stocks have done well over the last decade, this once again depends on how well you predicted the future. Among the biggest Blue Chip stocks names, IBM put in a solid performance, rising from $100.15 to $182.60 over the ten year period.

This gives it an 82.3% gain through early August, for 8.23% per year. Citibank declined horribly from $462.50 to $39.34, falling 91.5%, a loss of 9.15% per year. McDonald's put in a solid decade, rising from $30.23 to $87.49 over the decade. This makes it among the best performing major stocks at up 189%, for 18.9% per year.

Why are these Investment Returns Even Worse When Adjusted for Inflation?

So it is fair to say that you barely made any money if you followed Wall Street's advice and diversified into a broad basket of stocks like the S&P 500, or even the Dow Jones Industrial 30. Broadly representative mutual funds mostly performed at the same lackluster level. A few individual stocks did alright, and others were destroyed like the bank stocks.

This is not the end of the story where Wall Street stock returns are concerned. On top of the literal returns, you have to take into account inflation over the time frame from Sept. 2001 to August 2011. The U.S. inflation calculator tells you that inflation has risen 28% during this time period, or 2.8% per average year.

Why Does This Matter at All?

Because what your dollar bought in 2001 now costs you $1.28. You have lost 28% of your purchasing power, or 2.8% per year. So if you made .9% gains in the S&P 500, then you have actually lost almost 2% per year. The DJIA with its 1.8% return per year lost you a full percent per year adjusted for official inflation numbers.

The NASDAQ is the only major average that would have made you money over the last ten years, with its 5.5% a year return that drops to 2.7% after inflation. Remember that this inflation figure is only the official government inflation number, and not the real inflation levels that many economists admit are actually significantly higher. According to Shadowstats.com the real inflation rate is about 11% right now.

Will you trust your broker's claims that Wall Street makes you great returns over the long term or your own intuition that is now backed up by the cold, hard facts?

DRIPs - An Overlooked Stock Investment Opportunity

When you think about great opportunities in the stock market, DRIPs are probably not the first things that pop into your head. DRIPs are more than just a clever acronym that sounds like a leaky faucet.

They represent the most overlooked stock investment opportunity in the market today. In the paragraphs below, you will learn all about DRIPs in general, as well as about a few different solid stocks that pay good dividends and participate in the DRIPs program.

What Are DRIPs?

You should know that DRIP stands for Dividend Re-Investment Plans. Companies offer these programs to existing shareholders in the company so that you are able to purchase additional shares of stock straight from the company that issues the stock itself. You are able to eliminate the middle man this way.

You also gain the ability to purchase from enormous numbers of shares of stock to tiny amounts of shares. This program can be set up to invest money on an annual, semiannual, quarterly, or even monthly basis.

DRIP plans also offer you the convenience to re-invest a portion or all of the dividends that you receive into additional shares of the stock. This helps to explain the clever name of Dividend Re-Investment Plan, or DRIP.

What Are the Different Kinds of DRIPs?

There are three types of DRIPs that you can participate in when you search for these stock investment plans. A great number of them are run by the companies that issue the stock directly. They often permit you to purchase shares from them even if you do not already own any of their stock.

Corporate headquarters run the DRIP under the shareholder and investor relations operations. There are even companies that will offer their own IRA, or Individual Retirement Account, plan as a part of the DRIP program.

Other DRIPs are run by transfer agents. Those companies that are overwhelmed by how complex it is to manage their own DRIP have sought out professional third party help of transfer agents.

This makes the stock company's life much easier. You benefit in this case because a transfer agent is typically a financial institution that operates DRIPs for many different corporations. This means that they are able to use economies of scale to offer you the plan at a far less expensive rate than one company would be able to do on its own. Among the biggest transfer agents are Chase Mellon, First Chicago Trust, and Boston EquiServe.

Still other DRIPs can be set up through stock brokerages. There are stock broker houses that permit you to take advantage of DRIPs and the dividend reinvestment part of the program with no fee.

They do this even when the corporations themselves do not offer such a DRIP.

The downside to these types of DRIPs is that you can only take advantage of the dividend re-investment option. This means that in these types of DRIPs, you are not able to make direct cash purchases of the company stock, as you might with an OCP, or Optional Cash Purchase Plan.

What Are the Advantages of DRIPs?

There are many advantages when you choose to go with a DRIP. These DRIPs permit you to make the most effective use of your stock dividends. You can put your money back to work in the company, rather than gain less than a percent or two interest in a money market account or than simply fritter away the dividend checks on the weekend. Practically every DRIP will permit you to do the dividend re-investment at no charge.

Another great feature of DRIPs is this Optional Cash Purchase plan. Many DRIPs will permit you to buy additional shares for as little as ten dollars per month. Although all of them have limits to how many extra shares that you can purchase every quarter, these usually allow you to sink up to thousands of dollars per quarter into additional shares with no stock broker commission charge and little to no other fees.

DRIPs are like a savings plan that puts your money to better use than a simple checking, savings, or money market account. While such rival accounts pay a paltry sub one percent to several percent rate, with stock shares in good companies in a DRIP, you gain the benefit of a dividend.

You also get to capture price appreciation with these additional shares as the companies' earnings and profits grow over time. These plans force you to save money, since they deduct from your accounts automatically.

Nowadays, there are in excess of one hundred different firms that offer DRIPs that permit you to buy stock in the company at a lower price than the price offered on the major stock exchanges. Such purchase price breaks vary from a single percent to even a ten percent discount.

When you purchase shares this way, you already have profits on your stock share investment. Even if there are fees to start the DRIP or to purchase the shares, this generous discount will generally cover them. There are also corporations that will only give you this discount on the share price when you buy the stock with your dividends, not with cash. This encourages you to re-invest your dividends in the company stock.

How Does Money Accumulate over time in DRIPs?

DRIPs build up money in your stock account over time exactly like water drip, drip, drips into a bucket. The amounts that go in on a regular monthly or quarterly basis may not be much. Your dividend checks may amount to only a few dollars. But over time, just as individual water drips will fill up a bucket, so too your constant barrage of money and dividend re-investments that you drip into the program will eventually amount to a significant holding of the company stock.

You are able to begin a DRIP program even if you do not have much money to start. Most DRIPS will permit you to enroll with only the purchase of a single share.

Besides this, if you build up a portfolio of stocks that pay decent dividends, then you are able to increase the value and holdings of your company stakes to the point where you receive significant dividend checks each month.

What Are Some Good Stocks to Consider for DRIPs?

There are many good DRIPs out there from which you can select. You might consider three solid companies in businesses that almost always seem to outperform. These include oil companies, computer technology companies, and consumer staples, such as fast food businesses.

Conoco Phillips, with a New York Stock Exchange symbol of COP, offers between a 3.75% to 4% dividend yield. The large American oil and gasoline company always seems to turn a profit, especially with higher oil prices. You can open a DRIP plan in this and other major companies for only a $250 minimum investment.

You find Intel on the NASDAQ stock exchange under the symbol of INTC. The computer chip industry leader has proven its ability to survive and even excel in challenging economic times. The dividend yield of 4.2% is impressive.

You may have even eaten in the restaurants of the third recommended DRIP plan company, McDonald's. Their success continues to be legendary, as they seem to make even more money in bad economic times than they do in prosperous ones. McDonald's dividends yield between 2.7% and 3%.

Can you think of a better way to force yourself into a savings plan that will actually pay you back with better returns than mere bank or money market account interest?

The Most Profitable Investment No One Talks About

These days, you are among the comfortable majority if you are looking for an investment that is both safe and profitable. The stock market in general is a roller coaster ride that is not for the faint of heart.

Treasury bonds do not pay enough for you to hold. Corporate bonds are fraught with the risk that the underlying company goes bankrupt. Even residential real estate has dropped anywhere from twenty to fifty percent throughout the U.S and many other Western nations in the last five years. Where should you turn?

There is an overlooked investment class that you can bank on in good times and bad. In the paragraphs below, you will understand what it is, who owns it, and why it almost always outperforms rival investment classes over time.

What is The Best-Performing Asset Class In America?

It may shock you to learn that the asset class that performed the best in the last forty years' time is actually farmland. The U.S. Government keeps statistics on this asset with the highest return over the last four decades.

From 1970 to date, such farmland has yielded an incredible average yearly return of 13.6%.

There is still more data on the returns that farmland provides. Iowa State University researchers have performed detailed studies on the values of farmland in America. According to tenured Economics Professors Don Hofstrand and William Edwards, the price appreciation and cash yield values for American farmland over the last fourteen years amounts to 497%, or an average of 35.5% per year.

More impressive still, farmland has not suffered a negative year since 1987. That year of the Black Monday stock market crash, farmland declined a mere 1.2%. In the time frame since 1992, farmland has given you a return of 11.2% per year on average.

Over that one specific twenty year time frame, farmland can boast to have outperformed both gold and the stock market. Farmland may be the only major investment class that has not suffered a negative return year in any of the past twenty years.

What Other Benefits Does Farmland Give You Besides Great Price Appreciation and Yield?

Farmland offers you more than just phenomenal price appreciation and yield averages. It acts like a hedge against inflation, in much the same way as precious metals gold and silver do. The reason for this is that farmland proves to be a hard asset, unlike paper money.

As the government prints more money, the price of farmland increases against the vastly more abundant, and therefore significantly less valuable, U.S. dollars. During the past sixty years, farmland has outperformed inflation, even when you do not take into account the income yield that the land creates each year.

On top of this, farmland creates income. This makes it a solid hedge against inflation that also provides you with decent cash flow. As strong as gold and silver are for investment and safe haven purposes, they do not pay you any money to hold them. This makes farmland somewhat unique.

Another advantage to farmland lies in its inherent characteristics as a negative correlation asset to typical investments such as bonds and stocks. Morningstar and the National Council of Real Estate Investment Fiduciaries both make this argument. As stocks and bonds fall, farmland prices rise. This means that you can bank on farmland as a defensive investment, even in the difficult economic days of today.

Who Has Already Invested in Farmland?

Farmland is not so well kept a secret as you might suppose. The super rich have already figured it out. They have invested in it for decades and in some cases for centuries. Consider some of farmland's long term owners, such as Lord Rothschild of Europe, Queen Elizabeth II of Great Britain, Wal-Mart founders the Walton family, and CNN, TBS, and TNT founder Ted Turner.

You also have the Ford family, Microsoft's Bill Gates, Amazon founder Jeff Bezos, the Hearst publishing family, and a significant portion of the members of the Forbes 400 list of the world's wealthiest people who are farmland owners. Even famous actors such as Julia Roberts, Harrison Ford, Val Kilmer, and Steven Segal own farmland ranches that they use for both profits and to obtain tax breaks. Val Kilmer's ranch in Santa Fe has earned him up to one million dollars per year in tourist business income.

It is not just wealthy business owners and celebrities who own and operate farmland and ranches. In just the last two years, you have seen both large institutional investors and hedge funds begin to invest in this area of great opportunity too. The California Public Employees' Retirement System is one pension fund that owns literally millions of acres of timberland. Yale and Harvard's university endowments are another two. The Teachers Insurance and Annuity Association have allocated two billion dollars for investments in farmland.

What Are the Reasons that Farmland Does So Well?

At this point, you might wonder why it is that farmland has outperformed the stock market, bond markets, and at points, even gold and silver markets. The reasons why farmland does so well are many. It is an easy to grasp concept that does not involve complex investments and risky financial instruments.

It has proven to be safe as a store of value.

Land will never default on you, cheat you, or take your money and flee to the Caribbean or Switzerland. Besides this, land historically has outpaced even violent inflation bouts throughout history.

Ultimately, you should understand that farmland has so well outperformed other major asset classes because the population in the U.S. has risen by more than fifty percent from 1970 to date. Because of this, agriculture has to provide for over three hundred million people now, versus the two hundred million in 1970. This drives demand for wood, food, meat, and dairy products.

As more Americans have demanded more meat, the strain on the farmland has only increased. While you might require three to four acres of land to feed twenty-five people who eat vegetables and grain only, the same twenty-five people need an incredible sixty-three acres of land to support their eggs and beef habits. This has placed enormous strain on the available farmland resources throughout America. No one makes any more land these days, as Mark Twain famously observed back in the 1800's. Greater demand and fixed supply nearly always leads to higher prices.

How Can You Invest in Farmland?

For a small investor like yourself, it is not so easy to purchase farmland in any of its direct forms. If you have a significant amount of money stashed away, you might purchase a smaller farm. Ranches cost serious money. Another way to invest in farm, ranch, or timber land is to find a publicly traded company that focuses on the ownership and production of these assets. You can purchase stock in one of these companies if you really believe in its business model and holdings.

Alternatively, you can purchase bonds in these corporations that own farmland, ranch land, or timber land. If you acquire a bond, then you only make a loan to this company. They pay you a generous interest return that might amount to five or six percent each year.

It does not matter if the company has losses or profits, so long as they can make the interest and principal payments on their bond debts to you. If they do go out of business, then you are considered to be a top priority creditor who will be paid back from the value of their farmland resources when they are sold. Either way, you will come out ahead.

Now that you know how well farmland has performed over the last forty years, can you think of a good reason not to get involved with the most profitable investment that no one talks about today?

MINDSET

"Changing Habits, Attitudes and Intentions"

Mindset

Find Your Strategy to Build Wealth With a Personality Test

When you were growing up, you probably heard the old expression to do what you love and the money will follow. The sad truth is that too many people do not take this seriously. You grow up and abandon your dreams to instead pursue a career that offers job security and prospects.

There is a website and product that argues just what your elders used to tell you. Wealth Dynamics is a system that can teach you what your passion is so that you can learn to make money the natural way. In the article that follows you will come to understand the paths to wealth and how this system can show you the right one for you personally.

About Roger Hamilton

Roger Hamilton is the founder and designer of the Wealth Dynamics system. His Wealth Spectrum Test that is a part of this system has already helped literally tens of thousands of entrepreneurs in more than fifty different countries to find their area of natural flow.

His mission statement and that of his group World Wide Wealth is to increase the wealth flow for both individuals and adherents as a collective.

In support of this mission, Roger Hamilton has been on a continuous speaking circuit to spread the message of efficient wealth creation to more than two hundred thousand entrepreneurs living in fifteen different countries.

Besides This Wealth Dynamics system, Roger Hamilton has set up several other companies. He established Phi Dynamics. He also co-founded the XL Group and XL Nation.

What Are Wealth Dynamics?

You may think like numerous individuals today that hundreds of paths lead to wealth. According to Wealth Dynamics, there are merely eight different means to get there. One of these routes is the best one for your personality. People who have been most successful in life are the ones who determined which of these wealth dynamics best fit their abilities.

What Are the Eight Different Wealth Profiles?

Mechanics

If you like to create systems that can be easily duplicated, then you are a mechanic. These mechanics prefer to complete tasks instead of to start them. You enjoy perfecting products or services, like Ray Krock with McDonald's, Michael Dell with computers, and Henry Ford with his assembly lines for cars.

Creators

You who are creators enjoy putting together new and innovative ideas and products. You are successful when you design businesses and concepts that make money, but you are not good at day to day operations. Walt Disney, Steve Jobs, and Richard Branson are all good examples of successful creators.

Supporters

Those of you who are full of enthusiasm and energy and love to network are supporters. You can make a great amount of money if you team up with a creator, mechanic, star, or deal maker. Jack Welch and Steve Ballmer are banner examples of this wealth profile.

Stars

Stars are those who build up an important brand and excel in business, sports, music, and film. Business stars are well known and successful CEO's. Their personality is strong enough to take the high pressure that comes from having to deliver constant results. Bill Clinton and Paul Newman exemplify this type of profile.

Traders

Those of you who are traders love to find bargains, to hunt out deals, and to track down buyers who pay more. You are good at selling and buying commodities. Jim Rogers and George Soros champion this category.

Deal Makers

If you like connections and relationships, then you are a deal maker. You use these to locate the greatest opportunities available to you to turn them into success and make deals.

Rupert Murdoch and Donald Trump are classic archetypes of this wealth profile.

Lords

Lords are controllers. If you enjoy quiet success, then you are a lord. Lords employ fixed assets to create cash flow. Lakshmil Mital is such a type of individual.

Accumulators

You who like to find a system that works and stick with it are accumulators. You believe in incremental growth, as in to buy and hold a good asset or investment. Paul Allen and Warren Buffet are classic role models for this wealth dynamic profile.

As you can see, these eight profiles did not come about overnight. Roger Hamilton looked at hundreds of wealthy success stories in order to come up with them. He also studied and applied Chinese philosophy to the process.

What Does Wealth Dynamics Teach You About Yourself?

You will be surprised at the things that Wealth Dynamics can teach you about yourself. For starters, you do not have to suppress your natural passions and strengths in order to create wealth. Proof of this lies in the fact that the world's wealthiest people continue to pursue their occupations even when they can afford to stop.

When you are able to optimize your natural talents and activities that you find to be fun, then you will succeed. This will allow you to maintain the focus and energy level to see through the hard times.

All of the eight wealth strategies challenge individuals and sift out those who are only after money. This is one of the most important lessons of the Wealth Dynamics system.

How Does Wealth Dynamics Show Your Strengths?

The way that Wealth Dynamics works is through a system that profiles you according to the wealth category that you fit. It does this in a psychometric test. The test's goal is to asses you as a person, your strengths, personality, values, productivity, etc in order to find the way that is most natural for you to build wealth.

Before Roger Hamilton created this test, you had to resort to re-peated trial and error in order to learn the profile that fit you best. This could mean that you made a fortune with business but lost it in the markets. It might alternatively result in all your hard work to support someone else that made you a great amount of money being wasted when you opened your own business and it failed.

The Wealth Dynamics system makes it possible to remove these costly trials and errors from your path. It offers you the road map for your personal route to riches. It does this as it helps you to find the best strategy to follow. It also provides six steps for you to understand and enact in your own life.

Why Is This Important To Know Your Strengths?

The reason that you must know your own strengths is that you can only concentrate on one or two endeavors at a time in your limited hour days. This is the reason that Wealth Dynamics is so successful. No one wants to work with individuals who are only average at lots of activities.

They prefer to deal with those who excel at their one area of specialty. With the Wealth Dynamics system, you gain the ability to concentrate and specialize better. This way, you can focus on those activities that you like and are good at in order to succeed.

How Much Does Wealth Dynamics Cost?

The good news is that the Wealth Dynamics product is affordable. It costs you one hundred dollars to take the test and learn which wealth profile is idea for you. The time investment is also minor. In twenty minutes time, you will complete the assessment and learn which type of profile you are.

The system will then show you how to best succeed at your personal wealth profile. How can you go wrong when you learn what you are good at and where you can most effectively apply yourself?

Wealth Dynamic Profile:
www.wdprofiletest.com

The Spectrum Test - Your Path Towards Wealth Creation

If you have ever wished that there was a way to learn where you are on the path towards wealth creation, you now have a test you can take that will show you a level that applies to you personally.

This is called the Wealth Spectrum Test. The following paragraphs consider the various levels of this test and give you an idea of where you can expect to be placed when you take this test for yourself.

What is the Wealth Spectrum Test?

Roger James Hamilton designed the Wealth Spectrum and the test that accompanies it. He investigated the obstacles and opportunities that literally hundreds of thousands of different entrepreneurs who live in more than twenty nations experience to come up with this spectrum and its levels.

During his discovery, Roger learned that individuals can be placed into one of nine easy to understand levels on their wealth. Because he saw that individuals who worked at wealth at an inappropriate level for themselves achieved terrible results, he came up with the test and nine levels of wealth creation. These nine levels are organized into three prisms along color lines. When you take his test, you will learn which level you are at and how you should work to get to the next level.

The Foundation Prism Levels of the Wealth Spectrum

The first three levels of wealth lie in the Foundation Prism. You must master these levels about personal cash flow before you attempt to move on to manage investments and businesses. These first levels are Infrared Level Victim, Red Level Survivor, and Orange Level Worker. You can not help anyone else until you move above these levels that are necessary to take care of your own personal finances. These foundation levels are most critical to learn and surpass.

The Infrared Level, or victim, is easy to understand. You are here if you find yourself in financially worse shape each month than the last month. You sink further and drown in increased debt. This level finds you in a negative cash flow position and with negative trust from your peers. You will have to learn to budget your money and take responsibility for your finances in order to escape from this level.

The Red Survivor Level is the one where you realize only enough income to pay your bills. You can only get by if you stick strictly to your budget. This level means that money is a continuous restriction in your life. To escape from this level, you will have to find your passion and then link up with a team that makes money in order to generate additional cash flow.

The Orange Worker Level has you in a job where you work for someone, and you have work that gives you both satisfaction and good prospects to advance. This is the first sustainable level. So long as you continue to work effectively for others, you will be able to provide for your family. This level will not have you retire comfortably or wealthy.

To advance to the next prism and level, you have to understand your value in the production chain of your company and learn to control the cash that you generate in your position.

The Enterprise Prism Levels of the Wealth Spectrum

You find levels four, five, and six in the Enterprise Prism. To be in these levels, you must master control of cash flow in your business and investments to a point. The levels here are Yellow Player Level, Green Performer Level, and Blue Conductor Level. You find yourself in these levels of this prism if you look to start a company, to more effectively manage a business, or to gain additional resources in your self employed venture. All entrepreneurs and investors must learn these levels to succeed.

You are a Player once you reach the yellow level. This means that you keep busy on one instrument. If you are self employed, then you work with other individuals in your business. You can live at this yellow level comfortably, and you have the freedom to choose what you do. Along with this comes the responsibility to make money every month. You will master a role at this level, but you will always be busy. To move on to the next level, you will have to establish what your business will excel at and move along the steps of effective enterprise.

The second level in the Enterprise Prism is the Green Performer Level. You are in the green level when you rely on teams who also rely on you for their livelihood in your businesses and investments. You carry a heavier load of responsibilities at this level, and you also have high expectations from your team members.

The reward of this level lies in the fact that you construct an enterprise whose value can increase with each day. You can grow into a multi-millionaire as the owner of one or more small businesses or solid investments that you manage personally and effectively.

When you find yourself in the Blue Conductor Level, then you are an active investor or larger sized business owner. You have attained the level to build up cash flows that best fit your personality. Once you reach this level, your own daily expenses are now a small portion of the cash flow that you oversee.

Daily costs are not a worry for you as you are focused on the overall cash flow of your businesses and investments. Once you reach this level, you do not have to be afraid to lose everything that you have worked for any longer, since your personal finances are well situated to outlast any economic catastrophe or setback. This is the level of multi-millionaires who may find their personal fortunes even in the hundred of millions.

The Alchemy Prism Levels of the Wealth Spectrum

The highest group of levels in the Wealth Spectrum Test is the Alchemy Prism. The three levels in this group are the legendary wealthiest people in the world. They make the rules of the money creation game. In the past, these were emperors and kings.

Nowadays, individuals themselves can aspire to the levels that governments alone filled until recently. When you reach the Blue Trustee Level, the Indigo Composer Level, or the Violet Legend Level, then you can act in this capacity.

It is true that each entrepreneur has the potential to make the rules that every one lives by today. Very few individuals reach these levels.

These slots are filled by the likes of billionaires Richard Branson and Bill Gates. Individuals such as these are able to effortlessly create money. They make markets and commodities. The wealth of such billionaires is not limited to or held hostage by any single country or its policies. They use the power of all the levels and many individuals. Work for those who deal in billions is never about the money. They are able to create cash simply by licensing out their name or brand for literally millions.

Why would you not want to take the Wealth Dynamic Spectrum test to learn which level you are in and how you can achieve the higher levels in your own life?

Take the test and find out where you are on your path of creating wealth. www.wdspectrumtest.com

How to Overcome The Parkinson Law for Financial Success

If you have ever heard the expression that your work expands to fill the amount of time that you have available, then you may have wondered where such a true observation originated. This all too true saying is one of many statements today that is based on the work of Cyril Northcote Parkinson.

Cyril Parkinson developed a law that has been applied to countless situations, from bureaucracy in business and government, to work and time in general. In the paragraphs that follow, you will understand how his law applies to your daily life and finances and why you must work to overcome its potent effects on a daily basis if you are to succeed.

Who is Cyril Northcote Parkinson?

Cyril Northcote Parkinson is a well known British author of around sixty books. While most of his works centered on naval history and fiction, he achieved undying fame for his bestseller work "Parkinson's Law." As a result of the success and critical acclaim of this book, he is considered to be a significant contributor in the area of public administration.

Apart from the intuitive brilliance of his Parkinson's Law that he formulated, Parkinson's educational background deserves your respect. He received a scholarship to study history for his undergraduate years at Cambridge University. After he earned his BA degree in the year 1932, he went back as a graduate student to King's College London.

His Ph.D. doctoral thesis won the Julain Corbett Prize for Naval History in 1935. Parkinson's Law has been praised by the Italian Alessandro Natta, as well as by the Soviet Union's final leader Mikhail Gorbachev, who pointedly observed that his law applies everywhere.

What is Parkinson's Law?

Parkinson's Law has been defined in many different ways by various individuals over the years. He first explained it in an well known essay found in a 1955 edition of "The Economist" by saying that work expands to fill up the available time for its completion. This is not his full law as he expounded on it later, but it has become a well recognized truth.

Parkinson's full law actually states that an organization's number of administrators will expand at a consistent rate regardless of the quantity of work that the organization actually has to complete.

Cyril Parkinson explained this in great detail out of his personal experiences as a civil servant in Great Britain in the book of the same title, "Parkinson's Law." As a civil servant, Parkinson keenly observed something interesting about the British Colonial Office.

Even though the number of colonies that this office had to administer declined continuously throughout the nineteen forties, fifties, sixties, and seventies, at the same time, their number of employees steadily increased. The irony of this fact is that when the Colonial Office was folded into the Foreign Office because they no longer had any colonies to manage, they employed more people at this point than when they had the most colonies to manage.

Parkinson's Law filled an entire volume with this examination of how the British Colonial Office experience could be correlated to organizations that included not only government but business as well. With sharp comic wit and imaginative genius, he employed the analytical tool to examine the problems with businesses and government.

It is more than just a casual observation that many typical practices in both government and business simply do not pass the test of common sense. Parkinson took the opportunity to make fun of plush offices, too many managers, numerous big meetings, aggressive schedules, leadership that was insecure, spend thrifts, micro managers, usual means of hiring, and other ridiculous mainstays of large business, government, and other organizations.

Parkinson extended this law to apply to administrative councils and their notorious lack of efficiency. He came up with a coefficient number of inefficiency that applied to these bodies. The number of sitting members is the main variable that determines the inefficiency of an administrative council.

How is Parkinson's Law Applied To Relevant Situations In Today's World?

Parkinson's Law is such a universal truth that it has been expanded beyond his original intent with great success and popularity. For example, his law is expressed as it pertains to time. A task will take as much time to finish as there is time allotted to complete it.

Since any task can easily grow to fill up whatever time you give to do it, you can reduce the amount of wasted time in your daily tasks by only allocating the needed amount of time to finish the task. Another way to put this is that if you leave something for the last minute, then it will only require a minute for you to accomplish it.

This time related application of Parkinson's Law also spawned several new interpretations of it with computers that are universally recognized. In this regard, his law is expressed as follows: data will expand to fill up the amount of storage space that is available for use. It is also sometimes said that the requirements for storage will grow to fill all available storage capacity. You may be familiar with another variation on the versatile law that states nature detests a vacuum.

What is Parkinson's Second Law and How Does It Relate to Your Personal Finances?

Parkinson is also attributed with a second law that has enormous relevance for your personal finances. This is often called Parkinson's Second Law. It states that your monthly expenditures will invariably rise to equal your monthly income. Another way to put this is that demands on resources will always rise to match available supplies of any given resource.

You can see how Parkinson was way ahead of his time with this second law. You know how true this is personally in your own daily life. If you simply leave money in your checking account, it has a way of gradually disappearing as all the bills are paid. The bills seem to expand as if by magic to absorb all of the excess cash that sits in your account. This is why you have to aggressively contend with this law on a monthly basis if you wish to have any money to save and invest.

Parkinson's Law in Action

The easiest way to make sure that you do not become a victim of Parkinson's Second Law is to set up a separate direct deposit with some of your weekly or monthly payroll through your employer. This deliberate action on your part to pay yourself ten percent first is the best remedy to this universally true pitfall. The separated money can go directly into a savings account, or better yet, into a high yield interest money market account. From here, you can move this money on in to investments that will earn you still better returns.

There is no real reason for you to fall prey to Parkinson's Laws. You can manage both your time and your finances effectively if you are only aware of the dangers that these two aphorisms so accurately express. Is there a better way that you can think of to stretch your money than by taking a portion of it out to segregate it away from the greedy bills that always expand to fill the void in your account?

Five Steps You Must Take Not to Become a Financial Sheep

You may have heard the saying that one percent of the people make all of the events in the country, while nine percent of individuals follow these events, and the other ninety percent pay no attention to them at all.

Where your finances are concerned, you simply can not afford to become a financial sheep along with the overwhelming majority of other people out there.

The good news is that you do not have to wander the financial wastelands with the crowded masses in these difficult economic times that only seem to be getting worse. In the subsequent paragraphs, you will learn the five financial steps that you have to take to maintain your financial independence in a shaky economic world.

Step # 1 - Do Not Entrust your Money to a Financial Adviser or the Wall Street Financial Firms

The vast majority of people give their money to someone to manage it for them. Your 401k, IRA, and other investment account are not alone if they reside with a financial adviser or one of the larger or smaller Wall Street firms. The problem with this practice lies in the fact that neither your financial adviser nor any of the Wall Street firms actually has your best interests at heart.

Their goal is simply to make money for themselves and their companies. Since they are rewarded based on sales and profits that these financial products generate, you can count on them to act in their own best interests over yours most every time.

Even if you did find a compassionate financial adviser who thinks first about your money and future, you will still pay enormous fees to these individuals and their Wall Street companies. Over twenty to thirty years' time frame, the average retirement account pays in the neighborhood of $250,000 to $300,000 in fees, commissions, and other charges.

Instead, you must take charge of your own financial future. You need to work on your financial education every day that you can. Once you start to read financial publications such as "The Wall Street Journal," "Barron's," or "The Economist," you will have a solid handle on what economic and political events should influence your own financial decisions.

Read good investment books that you can buy from a bookstore or borrow from your library. You might even attend some investment education seminars, workshops, or even area college classes. Before long, you will gain confidence in your abilities and be ready to manage your own money.

Step #2 - Build Up Passive Income and Precious Metals Investments

Despite the recent Standard and Poor's downgrade of U.S. government debt, interest rates remain at historic low levels for the present. Now is the time to borrow money aggressively for good debt. Good debts permit you to obtain investments that pay passive income to you over and above the cost to finance your debt.

You might obtain real estate investment trusts, oil and gas trusts, rental income properties, or even safe and defensive high yield dividend stocks that pay in excess of five percent dividends every quarter.

You should also not neglect some safe haven diversification of your low interest funds. You can invest in gold and silver through Exchange Traded Funds on the stock exchanges with GLD and SLV. You can also purchase physical holdings of either metal and store them in a safe deposit box or in your own safe at home. Either way, you will be protected from the wild financial swings that will inevitably lead to inflation and additional money printing activities in the U.S. and global economies.

Step #3 - Do Not Pay off your House Mortgage - Use the Money Instead to Buy Gold and Silver

If you have worked hard and saved up enough money to pay off the mortgage on your house, then you are fortunate. This is what many financial analysts will tell you that you should do--- pay off your debt. The truth is that your home mortgage most likely has a low fixed interest rate attached to it. You could not borrow this money so cheaply though any other vehicle such as credit cards, lines of credit, or bank loans.

This is why you should use this money wisely to acquire assets that have real, tangible, proven, historical value. There is no better place in the world you live in today for you to put this money than in the two precious metals gold and silver. You can always soldier on with your mortgage payments. If the economy continues to crumble in the coming years, then you will be far happier with the gold and silver that you own than for the house that you might have paid off.

Step #4 - Withdraw the Money from Your 401k and Invest in Silver and Gold

In the hard economic times that are on us, you should not leave your retirement money at the mercy of the stock market. Do not be fooled by the notion that the stock market always outperforms other investments over the long term. In the Great Depression in 1929, the markets crashed. They actually rebounded over the next thirty-six months.

Just when investors let down their guard and believed that the impressive stock market hey-days had returned, the markets burned down to ash from which they did not fully recover until more than ten years later. Citibank has been watching a set of scary charts for the last few years. They have commented in the past that today's market looks eerily similar to the one of the Great Depression.

Do not be fooled into thinking that the markets have rebounded and everything will be alright. Now is the time to cash out whatever you have left in your 401k and use the money to invest in gold and silver. You may take a tax and penalty hit of twenty percent or more on the withdrawal, but this is far better than a potentially fifty to seventy percent drop in the markets over the coming years.

Step #5 - Prepare yourself for Financial Collapse over the Next Two Years

There are many different best selling authors and economists who are warning you of a dire economic collapse in both the United States and to a lesser degree in the entire West in the next two years.

Robert Wiedemer in his groundbreaking book "Aftershock," David Scarica in "The Great Super Cycle," Porter Stansberry in his Stansberry and Associates videos, and others have a lot of credibility from their predictions of the housing crash and financial crisis. You should consider the very real possibility that they are right, and take steps to protect yourself and your family.

This does not mean that you have to invest all of your money in can goods and a shrink wrapping machine, or in a bomb shelter out in Colorado. It does suggest that you should work to create a situation where you live as independently from the daily requirements of government handouts and society as possible.

You might put together an emergency supply of food, have emergency plans ready, grow your own garden, and take other practical steps that make sense in the event of any emergency or natural disaster. Not only will you sleep better at night, but you will find that you live healthier as a result of fresh fruits and vegetables and a simpler way of life.

Do you want to be among the ten percent of people who make things happen and are aware of what is going on in the world, or a victim like the ninety percent who simply do not care?

The New National Disease - The Government Should Provide

You may have heard that there is a new national disease that is stalking the citizens of America. This disease is that the government should provide everything for you. The plague has been growing and spreading around the nation over the last few years on a frightening scale to the point that nearly half of Americans suffer from it now.

The truth is that your government was never intended to provide you with anything except for justice and defense. In the paragraphs that follow, you will be able to discover if you have this government dependence disease as you learn about the major symptoms of it, like the payment of no taxes, the receipt of food stamps or other government benefits, and government jobs.

What Percentage of Americans Pay No Taxes at All?

On July 7 of 2011, Texas Republican Senator John Cornyn made an incredible statement in a Senate floor speech on the subject of how few Americans actually pay Federal income taxes. He said that the Committee on Joint Taxation states that fifty-one percent of all American households did not pay any Federal income taxes at all in 2009.

Even more shocking was the fact that thirty percent of all American households not only paid no taxes, but they also received money back in the form of refundable tax credits.

This means that almost one in three Americans made money on the tax system. This amounts to nearly one hundred and fifty million Americans who pay no income taxes and ninety million Americans who paid negative income taxes, or received money in taxes.

How is it possible to not only pay no taxes but to make money in today's American tax system? Many Americans find that all of their tax liability is canceled out by tax credits. These include The Making Work Pay tax credit that President Obama established to redistribute the wealth from richer Americans to those who barely get by, as well as the Earned Income Tax Credit that helps lower income Americans who work to receive additional money. By the time these tax credits are figured up and applied, a mere forty-nine percent of Americans paid any income taxes at all to the Federal government in 2009.

This is a mind boggling statistic, but it is true. You may wonder who pays all of the taxes that are collected then? For the year 2007, the Urban-Brookings Center demonstrated that the wealthiest twenty percent of Americans paid nearly sixty-nine percent of all Federal government taxes. At the same time, the highest one percent of American earners paid over twenty-eight percent of all U.S. government taxes. The statement that more than half of the U.S. population has the Government Dependency Disease is hard to argue with in light of these unbelievable numbers.

What Percentage of Americans Receive Food Stamps?

A smaller but still incredible percentage of Americans receive more material help than just money back from the government every month.

According to the National Inflation Association, the Federal government gives more than forty-four million U.S. persons some type of food stamps to ensure that they can afford the basic necessities at the grocery store every week. To put this number in perspective, it represents around fifteen percent of the entire country. This means that almost one in five Americans now counts on direct government support to purchase food.

What Percentage of Americans Receive Social Security or Disability Benefits?

It will also stun you to learn how many Americans are on the Social Security and Disability Benefits dole here in the U.S. The Social Security Administration says that for 2011, almost fifty-five million Americans will get $727 billion in Social Security, disability, and survivor benefits.

Who is receiving all of this money, and how does this break down? Retirees make up thirty-five million of the total and receive $40.7 billion. Their dependents number almost three million and get $1.7 billion. Workers who are disabled make up eight million individuals who count on $8.8 billion each year.

Disabled dependents total two million people who get over half a billion dollars. Survivors tally about six and half million individuals who get $6.3 billion. All told, these categories add up to in excess of eighteen percent of the U.S. population. Almost one in five residents of the U.S. counts on money from the Federal government every month to pay their bills.

Between food stamps and cash benefits such as social security and disability payments, one in three Americans lives with The Government Dependency disease.

What Percentage of Americans Work for the Government Directly or Indirectly?

These numbers are high enough to convince you that the country suffers from a terrible disease of government dependence. A third of Americans live on government handouts, while a third of Americans receive money in taxes from the government, and more than half do not pay any part of the Federal income tax bill. The last symptom and category of Americans who depend on the government are those work work for the government either directly or indirectly.

The U.S. Bureau of Labor Statistics says that government jobs only account for around eight percent of jobs that exist in the United States. This does not count all workers on the government payroll by a long shot though. Non post office, Federal civilian employees number 1,774,000.

The Post Office has 615,000 employees on its roles. The military counts 1,403,490 enlisted and officer personnel. State government employees not counting hospital or education sectors number 2,424,000. The local governments not counting hospital or education employee employ 5,594,000 total.

All of these categories combine for 11,810,490 state, local, and federal government jobs. This only makes up 7.84% of employees with 150,600,000 jobs in the U.S for the year 2006. It does not sound like so many.

There are actually many more people who work for the government directly or indirectly. New York University government professor Paul C. Light did a study on this. He determined that in 2006 there were also over fourteen and a half million contractors who work for the Federal government. These two categories total up to 17.5% of all jobs as government employees.

This figure still leaves out hospital workers, education workers, and state and local government contractors too. If you include all of these who are decisively dependent on one branch of the government, then the number rises to one out of every three workers, which makes up a full thirty-three percent of the population that works for the government.

Why Is It Not Alright to Have the Government Dependency Disease?

It is not alright to be a victim of this Government Dependency Disease. When you make another person responsible to provide for your needs, then you become a victim of circumstances. This horrible attitude takes responsibility away from you.

As a victim of this disease, you can be certain of one thing. You will never see any wealth materialize in your own life. Besides this, you can not forever count on a government that pays out more money in social programs than it collects in tax revenue. Is it not time to take your life in your own hands and stop trusting that the government will take care of everything for you?

3 Effective Methods to Overcome Your Financial Fear

Fear is your natural reaction to an unknown situation. Your mind tells your body that you are in danger and you must take urgent steps to protect yourself. The problem with this normal response to perilous stimuli is that it can paralyze you so much that you are unable to move or even decide on any course of action. Your mind's actions and reactions to financial decisions are no different.

When there is a possibility to lose some, or even possibly all, of your money that you invest, you can expect financial fear to be a real problem for upwards of ninety percent of the population. The good news is that you can overcome your financial fears, as you can with any type of rational fear that afflicts you in your own life.

In the paragraphs that follow, you will learn how you can follow three relatively simple and painless steps in order to make your financial fears a thing of the distant past.

What Is Financial Fear Really?

This type of fear arises when you begin to move into uncharted financial territories in your own life. This could be as a result of a decision that you make to start up a business or when you invest your own money in stocks, bonds, real estate, and other investments whose outcome is neither guaranteed nor necessarily assured.

Fear comes from intimate knowledge of the possibility that you might inadvertently make mistakes that cost you plenty and dearly. It is this fear of financial risk that plagues practically every investor who has not learned to master it. You must understand that risk is not something that you have to live in fear of; instead, it is an element that can lead you to success in your finances and even life in general.

The good news is that there is help to overcome this fear of risk and financial loss. Through education, mistakes that you make and learn from, and test runs, you can learn to grapple successfully with risk and to overcome your own very natural and real fear of financial failure.

Step Number 1: Education - Get As Much Information About Your New Task As Possible

The first weapon that you need to defeat financial fear is education. When you learn as much about the world of finance and investments as you can, you will find that you can beat down your financial fear demons much more effectively. It is the unknown that you are afraid of, after all. This is why it is critical to move the world of investments from the unknown to the known through solid financial education.

What types of education should you seek in order to begin to lay to rest your financial fear? There are many different avenues that you could and really should pursue. If you are a true novice in the world of investments, the best place to start is with a general all around guidance book like "Rich Dad, Poor Dad," by famed entrepreneur and self help writer and speaker Robert Kiyosaki.

It is hard to go wrong with the greatest and best selling financial self help book that has ever been published.

After you cut your financial teeth on this excellent all around work, you can move on to other more advanced books on the topics of investments, money management, and markets in general.

You should also take the time every week to read one or more good financial publications. There are so many of these that are available to you either in print by subscription or over the Internet. You could choose to read "The Wall Street Journal," "The New York Times," "Barron's," or "The Economist," as well as others out there.

Whichever you select, make sure that your financial comprehension skills are up to the level of the publication. It does you little practical good to proudly claim that you read "The Economist" religiously if you have no idea at all what the magazine talks about.

Lastly, do not overlook the opportunity to take continuing education courses to further your financial education and overcome your financial fear. Most local community colleges will offer classes ranging from the basics of money management to the intricacies of investments, finance, and economics.

You might also enroll in one or more seminars that pass through all of the major metropolitan areas of the country every year. These are offered on such topics as real estate investments, stock market investments, precious metals investments, and other sound financial and investment topics.

Step Number 2: Allow Yourself to Make Mistakes And Learn From Them

The next step that you must take once you acquire a solid financial footing through your education is to permit yourself to actually make mistakes. There is no shame when you make an investment that does not turn out so well as you hoped. The important point is that you must not waste the opportunity to learn from your financial missteps.

If you buy Apple stock at too high a price and it declines five or ten percent, it will not be the end of the world. Rather it will be a chance for you to learn the critical investment lesson that tells you to buy low and sell high. Similarly, if you purchase a residential real estate investment and the housing market continues to decline, then you might have to hold on to the property for a long time.

At least you could learn from the experience that you may rent out the property in order to bring in some positive cash flow and passive income while you wait for the price of the property to recover with time.

The point is that you are a human being and you will make investment mistakes as you practice. Even the renowned professional investors become involved in colossal blunders from time to time.

What separates the super wealthy from the rest of us is that they pick themselves up, dust themselves off, and continue to try something new and different in a smarter way the next time. Do not be afraid to learn from your financial mistakes.

Step Number 3: Do a Test Run Or Make A Small Step First

Finally, you should know that the smartest of investors do not throw caution to the wind, nor put all of their hard earned investment capital at risk on one single opportunity. Instead, you should engage in test runs or small steps when you try out new investment ideas. This begins when you track a possible investment with pretend money sometimes.

It might also mean that you put only a portion of your investment capital at risk on your big financial or investment idea. This is not a popular idea that you should keep some of your proverbial investment powder dry. Yet if you can learn to discipline yourself and follow it, then you will find that you consistently live to fight another day a whole lot better than your friends and family members who put all their chips on one single turn of the investment roulette wheel.

Why should you let fear of financial failure control you when you can overcome it in three simple steps?

Mindset

RETIREMENT

"Planing for Financial Freedom"

Retirement

Bank On Yourself - The Rapid Growth Retirement Program

When you look at your investment and retirement accounts these days, you probably do not like what you see. If the numbers on those page lead you to believe that you will never be able to retire by the time that you are sixty anything, then you need a new approach.

You can not argue that doing everything that the financial gurus like Jim Cramer, Suzie Orman, and Dave Ramsey suggested has led you to where you are today. If you do not make some sort of change quickly, then you will be in the same boat as literally millions of Americans when it is time for your retirement. You will have to work until the day when you draw your last breath just to cover your bills.

Wall Street has lost you and other investors forty-five percent of your hard earned investment dollars on two occasions in just the last decade. You can not be sure that they will not do this again. There is a website that offers you hope to save and achieve retirement that guarantees the most impressive results called Bank on Yourself. In the paragraphs that follow, you will learn how taking the advice found at Bank on Yourself can lead you to realistic hopes of retirement.

Pamela Yellen and Her Book 'Bank on Yourself'

Since the year 1990, Pamela Yellen has partnered with more than forty thousand different financial advisers in order to assist them in building up a sustainable business model. In this time, she has sifted through in excess of four hundred and fifty different financial tools, products, concepts, and methods that claimed to be the most effective means to increase your wealth. She came up with one system that can radically change your life, Bank on Yourself, in the course of her investigations.

The results of Pamela's investigations are published in her New York Times best selling book entitled, "Bank On Yourself." This book is not a silver bullet. It requires discipline and some patience for you to see some impressive results in your financial future.

Why should you listen to Pamela's advice in this ground breaking book? It has been the best seller on not only the New York Times, but also on USA Today, The Wall Street Journal, and Business Week. She has over two hundred approved Bank on Yourself agents who are now trained to help you. Pamela has also made guest appearances on all of the major television and radio networks in support of her ideas in this book and on the website of the same name.

These appearances include CBS, ABC, NBC, FOX, CNN, and National Public Radio. Her articles have been seen in literally hundreds of different major publications and website, such as Fortune Small Business and USA Today. In her professional speaking engagements, she has given speeches to in excess of one thousand audiences around the U.S., Europe, Asia, and Canada.

Her book is well endorsed by many of the most respected experts on wealth. If these accolades and accomplishments are not enough, Pamela Yellen has set up a challenge to give the first individual who successfully employs a competing strategy or product one hundred thousand dollars. She deserves your respect and attention.

What is Bank on Yourself?

Bank on Yourself is a system that shows you the means to increase your money both predictably and with safety. This works even if bonds, stocks, real estate, and other types of investments crater. The system works with a vehicle called a whole life insurance policy. To this, you add a few special features that are little known. The end result is that this product will easily trump your typical retirement plans and financial strategies.

Most people and even experts believe that in order to collect on a life insurance policy, you have to pass away. Yet there are real financial benefits to the policy that Bank on Yourself employs. When this policy is set up correctly, it will permit you to have a greater level of flexibility than any competing type of investment on the market.

It will also give you a higher level of security, guaranteed growth, and peace of mind than you have ever seen with a rival savings and investment program. If you need some big name endorsements of other successful individuals who utilized the Bank on Yourself strategies, consider that both J.C. Penney and Walt Disney worked with the method.

How Does Bank on Yourself Work?

Bank on Yourself uses a Whole Life Insurance Policy. In this form of life insurance, you get an annual increase amount that is determined and guaranteed by contract. If the stock market fails, your gains and principal are still both protected. The gains in such a policy are not only guaranteed, they are exponential. This simply means that the gains improve with every passing year when you stick with the policy.

On top of this, a number of insurance companies also pay out dividends to their policy holders. These may not be officially guaranteed, but in practice they often are implied. Such dividends have actually been made every year for longer than one hundred years by some of these solid companies, even when the Great Depression raged.

You are able to optimize the results of this Bank on Yourself program when you pair a whole life policy that pays dividends with two other features. They must include a rider that states that some of your money goes into rapid growth allocation. They must also permit you to borrow money that you pay into the policy so that you can cover expenses or invest in another vehicle.

The increase and dividends would continue even after you had borrowed these funds. What this means is that the Bank on Yourself Whole Life Insurance Policy is actually far superior to a traditional IRA or 401K plan. This is because you do not have to pay interest on any funds that you borrow from the policy.

Get Your Free Investment Analysis

The best thing about the Bank on Yourself plan is that you are able to obtain a free investment analysis on your individual circumstances without having to commit or put any money up. All that you have to do is go to the website. There you can find and click on the FREE ANALYSIS HERE button.

What is the Training Program About?

Bank On Yourself is also looking for additional Authorized Advisers to help other people make this program a part of their lives. The rewards include great satisfaction from assisting your customers in helping them to reach a financial security and peace of mind that they simply will not find otherwise. In order to qualify for the training program, you must have minimally a year of financial services experience and a life insurance license. You must also demonstrate the ability to be mentored and the right attitude to succeed in the program.

What is the Free Report that Is Offered?

The site also provides you with an offer for a free special report on how you can regain control over your financial picture. You can have immediate access to this eighteen page special report that is entitled, "How to Safely Grow and Protect Your Wealth, Even When Stocks, Real Estate, and Other Investments Tumble." This report also includes a monthly newsletter that would otherwise cost you $197 for the both.

When you have no obligation and nothing to lose, what is stopping you from trying out the Bank on Yourself system?

The 10 Best iPad & iPhone Apps For Retirement Planning

Retirement options are a concern of many Americans today. Planning for your retirement is one of the most important things that you can do. You need to start planning early to ensure that once you do retire you have enough funds to last you through the rest of your life.

You need to plan for unexpected expenses, any possible illnesses or emergencies that may occur and any changes in the economy.

The ability to manage retirement options while on the go has many iPhone and iPad users wondering, "Which retirement planning applications are the best?" The author discusses the 10 best applications in brief for the edification of the reader.

1. RetirePlan

Most users report RetirePlan as one of the best applications on the market. The graphs, spreadsheets and email capability increase the usability of the application. The application is free; so, it is also cost effective.

In just a few seconds you can enter your data and assumptions and the graph will update to show you if your plan will work. If you have more time to spend you can enter as much detail as you want to refine your plan.

The sliders give you an easy way to see what different values will do to your plan. Need to enter a value outside the slider range? press the amount and a calculator will pop up to let you enter whatever number you need. The slider range will update automatically.

Pros:

Easy to enter data, results are based on assumptions, sliders help users determine how different values will affect your retirement plan, spreadsheets include details for every year of the plan, email capability, capable of adding a spouse, pension, college, Social Security or inflation, excellent graphics, ability to add different rates of return or retirement assumptions.

Cons:

No Excel spreadsheet capability, no ability to toggle between charts listing current dollar value and how inflation affects retirement savings, no ability to determine how a market crash would affect the retirement value.

2. Retirement Dashboard

This particular application allows users to visualize the "value of savings against required retirement wealth." Users may determine the value of their savings in any type of market.

The easy input screen requires no training for you or your family to start to use Retirement Dashboard. And if you have any questions you can always reference the full glossary at a touch of a button. You can save all your scenarios for future reference. All saved reports can be accesses quickly. Retirement Dashboard has a clear report screen that enables you to view all the output of your calculations.

You can also email the report to family, friends or financial advisors at a touch of a button. This innovative application is available for $4.99.

Pros:

Easy input screen, intuitive and user-friendly, glossary for reference, easy-to-read reports for, viewing calculation outputs, excellent graphical charts, savable retirement reports, investment style types options, estimate value of wealth, capable of sending reports through text or email, supports multiple currencies.

Cons:

None

3. Retire Logix

Retire Logix is an innovative and interactive retirement planning application with sliders and charts for convenience. Users may change assumptions easily. Some assumptions include social security contributions, asset values, annual retirement spending, retirement age and inflation.

Retire Logix lets you split your retirement expenses into your Needs and Your Wants. The money you spend on your daily expense like groceries, household expenses, medical bills, insurance, are considered to be Needs. These are basic expenses you have to support in retirement.

Your Wants are anything you would like to plan for in retirement; things like travel expenses, entertainment, and other fun spending.

Pros:

Free, video Help option, data in application may be uploaded to Finance Logix Portal, retirement, time-line charts, easy to use and intuitive.

Cons:

Requires iOS 4.2 or later.

4. Guide to Retirement Planning

This guide helps users start their retirement plan by providing tips from start to finish. The comprehensive guide teaches you how to make the most of your employer's pre-defined retirement plan and make some adjustments to improve your financial outcome during retirement.

When was the last time you thought about what you would be doing in 10 years, 20 years, even 30 years? Probably not very often, huh? The thought of retirement planning probably isn't the most fun activity in the world. With the help of this book, You Can Easily Plan For Your Retirement! It contains more than everything you need to know to get started.

The guide is intended for a "how to" and may be used in conjunction with other applications. The cost is only $0.99.

Pros:
Helps users find free money in retirement plans provided by employers, teaches users how to invest in the stock market to improve retirement savings, teaches clients how to plan your will, instructs clients about health insurance and long-term care.

Cons:
Does not have the advanced features of other financial planning tools, guide is more instructional than calculations-driven.

5. Vanguard for iPad

Many retirement-age people seek a range of investments. Some people planning for retirement enjoy being in control of their investments.

Vanguard provides an application to help clients monitor their investments for retirement savings. Charts track the activity of stocks, Mutual funds, bonds and Exchange Traded Funds (ETFs).

Pros:

Perform mutual fund account transactions on your iPad, analyze the performance of your investments with charts and graphs, research investments online, view instructional videos and podcasts available through the application, share content through email, enables secure transactions.

Cons:

Not specific to retirement planning. Application primarily tracks investments. Does not have an application to factor in inflation or sliders to include different assumptions.

6. Fidelity Investments for iPad

This application allows retirement planners and investors to take charge of their own investment strategy. Fidelity's application addresses retirement-age people who are aware of the inflation factors and need a supplement to manage their investments. Through this application, clients may monitor market news and research investment opportunities.

You can view your brokerage and workplace savings accounts from virtually anywhere you are, with news, research, online bill pay, remote check deposit and other powerful tools right at your fingertips.

Pros:

Provides real-time market quotes, offers real-time market news, provides a list of the highest gaining stocks and the stock losers, monitors positions, funds transfers, balances and valuations of holdings, integrates with workplace savings information.

Cons:

Not specific to retirement planning. Application primarily tracks investments.

7. Market Dash

MarketDash from Yahoo! Finance provides easy access to your investment portfolios. Users have access to real-time quotes throughout the day. Clients may monitor all market movements by percentage, price or market cap while on-the-go.

Users are no longer confined to their desks.

Pros:

Stock market comparisons that may be viewed at a glance with interactive charts, real-time market information to help make stock picks, Manual refresh button for instant prices and updates, stock quotes may be easily added to watchlist or portfolio, double-click on the chart for a full-screen view.

Cons:

Not specific to retirement planning. Application primarily tracks investments.

8. The Street

This iPad application helps users analyze stock picks and view comments from investment experts on Wall Street. Technical analysis is instrumental to understanding how a particular stock will perform.

This is necessary for retirement investors that want to play an active role in their investment strategy.

Pros:

Includes numerous technical indicators that will determine ideal entry and exit points for stocks: Standard deviation, stochastic oscillators, RSI, MACD, CCI, Williams %R, Bollinger Bands, trend lines and others. Real-time stock market news, ETF and options experts. Videos include information about stock market data.

Cons:

Not specific to retirement planning. Application primarily tracks investments.

9. Retirement

The Retirement Calculator will help clients determine what they will need to plan a proper retirement for their clients. This application includes tools such as an IRA or Traditional IRA comparison calculator.

The application may also find quotes for all types of insurance that may be needed in retirement years. Annuities are important investment tools that ensure that people obtain an annual salary in their retirement years. Annuity rates are provided through the application.

Pros:

A Roth IRA versus Traditional IRA comparison calculator is included, an annuity planning calculator is included, insurance comparison calculator tools provides annuity quotes for comparison, a retirement planning calculator is included, an insurance comparison calculator can acquire insurance quotes from 10 different lines of insurance: health, renters, life, disability, long term care, cancer, burial, final expense and others.

Cons:

No specific retirement reports, no inflation calculations, reports cannot be saved.

10. Smart Money Retirement Planner

SmartMoney's Retirement Planner helps clients determine how their savings and spending habits will affect their retirement. Numerous scenarios can be tested. Whether you are concerned about Social Security or taxes SmartMoney's Retirement Planner can assist.

The application is free and allows the user to plan for him or herself or a spouse. Users will also learn how to optimize their savings for taxes. Tax havens may be found in certain retirement planning savings tools.

Pros:

Good inputs, quick estimating options.

Cons:

Does not remember or save settings, no capability to export or email output reports, data entry option requires too much effort.

Are You on Target to Reach Your Financial Retirement Goal?

Everyone is interested in retirement. The thought of not being forced to go to work to do a job that you quite possibly do not enjoy or that you are simply tired of is very appealing to Americans like yourself.

You might dream of the things that you can do when you actually have some free time, like travel, become more involved with clubs and hobbies, and even take occasional naps.

When you dream and scheme about what you will do when you reach retirement and how you will get there, you should take some serious time to think about how much money that you will need to actually retire. The answer to this question will depend on what you mean by the word retirement.

Will You Stop Working When You Retire?

The first question that you have to seriously ask yourself is how will you practically spend your retirement? Will you stop working completely, or simply shift over to doing a job that you would prefer to do instead? This is often called trading success for satisfaction. For many people like yourself, you will find that your satisfaction in retirement comes from working in a different field or on a schedule that is only part time.

You also might choose to go back and forth between points when you work versus points when you relax. A satisfying retirement for you should revolve around you finding ways to remain important, alive, and connected to other people. This new retirement concept also means that you will likely need to still make at least some money. This is especially the case since the glory days of pensions peaked in 1985, and they have been on the decline ever since.

Nowadays, a mere seventeen percent of people who do not work for some form of government entity can count on enjoying the traditional concept of a monthly pension check when they are retired. If you are not among them, then you should probably plan to continue with some form of work in your golden years.

You Will Have to Save More In Order to Completely Retire

You are likely in the comfortable majority of Americans who take advantage of their retirement plans that are based at work. Since eighty percent of workers engage in these, there are now more than forty-two million active participants in just 401K plans. These plans presently hold over thirteen trillion dollars worth of private and public retirement plan money. Even after the financial crisis and bear market of the last few years, this is still twice as much as what retirement plans held only ten years ago.

If you want to save the proper amount of money to be able to completely retire, then you should start working on saving an average of fifteen percent of your yearly take home pay while you are still young. This is the number that younger workers who are effectively planning ahead should strive to reach.

You should not become obsessed with this fifteen percent number when you save and invest money to retire. The idea is simply to save as much money as you are able to at the youngest age that you possibly can. This will see you on the right path and help you to make a solid start now.

If you manage to save fifteen percent of your gross salary, when you factor in contributions that employers match, then you should be able to replace fifty percent or even more of your salary in retirement. This will not get you all of the way to what you need though. And obviously, the later a start that you actually make, the greater amount of money that you will need to save each year.

From Where Will the Rest of the Money For Your Retirement Come?

Your ultimate goal is to have eighty percent of your income before retirement to replace your income with as you depart from your job. If you manage to come up with enough savings to reach fifty percent of it then this will not be enough. So where is the rest of the money supposed to come from for you to retire?

The hope is that you will realize as much as twenty to thirty percent of your important pre retirement income from social security. If you are an average wage earner now that possesses an income in the high thirties to low forty thousand dollars then social security will presently replace around forty percent of pre retirement income.

If you make more than this, then the amount it replaces is less. In either case this would increase your total for retirement to somewhere between seventy-five and eighty-five percent of the earnings that you are supposed to have in pre-retirement monies.

Hopefully social security will still pay out benefits at the present level in the future. This is not an assumption that you can count on though, which is why it is good to plan on working in retirement.

How Can You Possibly Save 15% of Your Earnings per Year?

This number of fifteen percent may sound like a huge amount of money that you can not hope to save by yourself. Once again, it is not all coming from only you. If you earn $40,000 per year and you contribute to your company 401K plan, then likely you are reaping the benefits of a match of fifty percent of your contributions to as much as six percent of your full salary.

This is the most common match in place in America today. You would need to contribute the full six percent to realize as much of the matching money as possible. This would amount to $2,400 per year. That would net you another $1,200 per year in employer match, bringing you up to $3,600 in contributions for the year.

Since contributions to 401K's are given in dollars before they are taxed, if you fall in a twenty-five percent tax bracket, then saving $200 per month means only reducing your take home pay by $150 a month.

As the employer would deduct this money before you ever saw it in your take home pay check, you would probably not miss it so much. That one action alone would help you to achieve greater than half of your goal for yearly savings and investment.

The remaining amount that you need to save would require you to add $2,400 per year to a retirement vehicle like an IRA or a Roth IRA. If you opted to use a Roth IRA, then you would not have to pay taxes on any of the withdrawals that you make from it in retirement.

As you are allowed to contribute more than this amount to either an IRA or a Roth IRA, you will not have any restrictions that stop you from maximizing your savings to the goal. So in the final assessment, putting aside $6,000 per year towards retirement would only require that you come out of pocket by the amount of $4,200.

What Experts Suggest You Should Have for Full Retirement

It is a good idea to be sitting down before you finish reading the article. Financial planners suggest that you really need to have a million dollars or more saved for retirement in order to generate a sufficient amount of earnings to provide you with the eighty percent standard of pre retirement dollars. Are you on target to reach this large number by the time you reach the age at which you wish to retire?

The 3 Different Types of Annuities For Your Retirement Goal

Annuities are a word that you hear mentioned when retirement options are discussed. This is especially true when you are talking with insurance companies. Annuities have their place for people who are planning for retirement.

This varies for every person and depends on what your particular retirement needs and plans actually are. There are different types of annuities that you should consider when you are laying out your retirement goals. The main types of annuities that are most appropriate for retirement are considered in the subsequent paragraphs.

What Exactly Are Annuities?

An annuity proves to be a contract that you make with an insurance company. In this arrangement, you either give the insurance company a number of payments over months or years, or you provide them with a one time large payment. For this consideration, they consent to provide you with routine payments starting on a certain date or a one time payout at a particular time.

Annuities have many attractive features that include growth that is tax deferred, and they often come with a death benefit that gives your beneficiary a minimal dollar amount. This is typically the amount of the principal that remains, and it can be be higher.

What Different Kinds of Annuities Are Available for Retirement Planning?

Three main types of annuities are used for retirement purposes. These are fixed annuities, variable annuities, and index annuities. Each of them has their own advantages and disadvantages. Some investors are better suited for one type of annuity than they are for another.

What Are Fixed Annuities?

A fixed annuity comes with a guarantee provided by the insurance company. They promise to provide you with a certain minimum interest rate while your account is in the first stage of accumulating and growing. The first year rate could be a bonus rate that is higher than the subsequent years.

Besides this, the insurance company promises that your payments will be a certain amount of every dollar actually in your account. There are two time frames of periodic payouts with fixed annuities. They can be for a set number of years and payments, as in fifteen or twenty-five years. They might also be for an unspecified period that covers you and your spouse until you pass away.

The interest that is earned on fixed annuities is clearly defined and pre arranged for a guaranteed number of years. After that time has elapsed, then you are given the choice to renew the interest rate at another rate that is guaranteed. Alternatively, you might surrender the annuity and take your money out, but this will cost you a fee. All annuities will include fees for death benefits and riders, as well as fees for options that you probably will not require.

The main downside to these types of annuities is that the funds are mixed into the general account of the insurer. This means that if the insurer fails, then your annuity payments will likely not be made and your principal can be lost. This is definitely something to consider when you pick out your insurance company, since it must be extremely solid and sound financially when you elect to have a fixed annuity.

What Are Variable Annuities?

Variable annuities permit you to choose where you invest your annuity balance. You are offered a variety of investment choices that are mostly different kinds of mutual funds. This means that your payments made into the annuity will have a return that depends on how well your chosen investments perform.

So the number of payments that you get will also vary with how well the mutual funds that you pick perform. These annuities segregate your funds from the general funds of the insurance company, which means that if the insurance company fails, your money will still be there.

Variable annuities give you the choice to make greater returns. If your chosen sub accounts that are tied to bonds, stocks, CD's, and other forms of investments do well, then you realize a certain percentage of this growth. The same death benefits that apply to fixed annuities and indexed annuities are applicable to these variable annuities too.

What is an Index Annuity?

Index annuities are specific kinds of annuities. As you are accumulating funds in the annuity with periodic payments or your one time deposit, the insurance company is providing you with a return that varies along with the changes in a particular index. This might be the S&P 500 or the Dow Jones Industrial Average.

With these types of annuities, your insurance company will usually promise you a minimum rate of return. Some of them come with principal guaranteed protection as well. When it is time for the distribution period, the insurance company pays out the annual, quarterly, and monthly payments as per the contract's terms. You might decide to get a one time payout from this kind of annuity as well. This makes these forms of annuities a hybrid, since they include elements of both fixed and variable annuities.

What Are the Other Important Differences Between the Three Types of Annuities?

The SEC actually regulates variable annuities, since they are considered to be securities. Fixed annuities on the other hand are not treated as investment securities and do not fall under their regulation. Fixed annuities are instead considered to be a combination of a life insurance policy and a bank Certificate of Deposit. Index annuities are treated as a combination of the two different types of variable and fixed annuities.

What Are the Retirement Benefits to These Annuities?

Any of the three kinds of annuities will permit you to earn interest and returns that grow tax free.

This is a substantial benefit over the years as you save for retirement. Plus, the three different kinds of annuities provide you with a good variety of choices to reach your retirement goals according to your personal risk tolerance.

For you who want to see tax free income growth that includes a consistent rate of interest that is as high as many money market accounts and also certificates of deposit, then there are special annuities that were created with you in mind. There are CD kinds of annuities, standard fixed rate annuities, or more conservative variable annuities that will permit you to invest your funds in CD's and bonds.

For those of you who have a goal of achieving greater returns that grow tax free, there are more ideal choices. You might put your money into a riskier variable account that typically pays better returns over the long term. This will allow you to select from the sub account investment choices that better match your risk profile and investment interests. The index annuities are another good choice if you are seeking higher returns and are comfortable with more risk.

What Are the Risks of Annuities?

Annuities have limited risks. Most of these are opportunity costs. If you go with a fixed annuity, than you risk making a lower return than you might have realized with a well chosen variable annuity or index annuity. When you select a variable annuity, you gain the opportunity to make the higher percentage returns, but you can lose some of your principal in most cases.

For many people planning for retirement, an index annuity may offer the most appropriate level of risk. This is because many of these can be obtained that guarantee your entire principal, even if your chosen index investment performs terribly. In this case, the risk would be that you do not make any interest on your money at all.

The real question that will get a different answer from each person is with how much opportunity cost risk are you comfortable?

ECONOMY

"Managing Resources for Prosperity"

Moody's Ratings Agency - The Last Falling Superpower?

New York Times columnist Thomas Friedman declared in a Jim Lehrer interview in 1996 that the two superpowers of the world are the U.S. and Moody's Ratings Agency, and you could not always tell which of the two were the more powerful.

Since Moody's started to threaten to downgrade the U.S. AAA national credit rating by putting it on credit watch review on July 13th, you have no doubt heard their name mentioned a great deal. Yet you still may wonder who is Moody's and why do they have this kind of power over entire countries. In the paragraphs below, you will learn what the purpose of Moody's is, how its infamous ratings function, and how reliable it is as an organization with such incredible power over companies and governments.

What it the Purpose of Moody's Ratings Agency?

John Moody created the practice of rating various securities back in 1909. He incorporated Moody's Investors Service on July 1, 1914. Municipal bonds were rated next. It only took ten years for the ratings provided by Moody's to extend to around a hundred percent of all bonds in the United States. Moody's continued to expand its ratings offerings in the 1970's.

They began to rate commercial debt and to charge the issuers of bonds for these ratings at that time. In 1975, Moody's only rated the debt of three countries. By the year 2000, this had grown to include over one hundred different nations.

The purpose of all of these ratings that Moody's offers is to give investors an easy to understand set of metrics with which to measure the credit worthiness of company and national securities.

In the capital markets today, these ratings aid the stability, expansion, and efficacy of both domestic and international markets. Investors are provided with the ability to assess risk on investments, while borrowers are able to determine what their funding terms will be in the capital markets. Economists, governments, savers, the media, and regulators all benefit from the ratings information provided by Moody's and its two principal rivals S&P and Fitch. Over eighty trillion dollars worth of fixed income and bond securities are now rated.

How Do Moody's Ratings Function?

Moody's reviews governments, companies, and investments and then assigns them a rating symbol. The idea is securities that share the same symbol have generally similar characteristics of credit worthiness. Moody's employs nine symbols ranging from the highly coveted AAA, to Aa, A, Baa, Ba, B, Caa, Ca, and C to express these levels of least risk to highest credit risk. Moody's further adds numbers one, two, and three to each of the ratings to further differentiate the issuers and their risk. Not every security, company, or government has a rating.

You should know that Moody's ratings can be changed at any given time. This is because the majority of issuers do not maintain consistent credit quality over the medium to long term. As their credit worthiness changes, so do the ratings that Moody's issues. This helps to ensure that the ratings actually reflect the risk inherent in the issuers and their instruments.

When Moody's considers changing the rating of an individual business or government, they go through a process. They give notice of a possible change in ratings by placing the issue on credit watch review. A ratings' change typically follows in the coming weeks or months. Bonds with lower ratings tend to see their ratings change more frequently than those with higher ratings.

How Independent is Moody's Ratings?

The issue of how independent Moody's Ratings actually are comes up all the time. Moody's is usually paid by the companies and governments that they cover to come up with these ratings. Naturally, this would encourage them to provide a satisfactory positive result in order to keep clients happy.

Moody's has over five hundred clients around the world, such as insurance companies, the biggest investment and commercial banks, mutual funds, financial service companies, utilities, manufacturers, technology and industrial clients, and governments on local and national levels.

Some outfits refuse to pay for ratings, and critics have leveled charges of blackmail against Moody's. German insurance company Hannover Re received free ratings offers by Moody's in the past. The company spurned the offer and refused to pay for future ratings. Moody's responded by keeping up the free ratings.

The problem is that they continuously cut Hannover Re's ratings with time. Hannover still refused to pay for Moody's services and subsequently saw Moody's cut their debt to junk status. It took only several hours for the market value of the insurer to plunge by $175 million as a result of this cut. No one will argue that Moody's is powerful.

Moody's is also considered to be extremely close to the banking industry that funds much of its annual earnings with their fees. They have been called gate openers for the banks instead of the gatekeepers that they are supposed to be. In 2007 alone, Moody's was forced to downgrade over five thousand different mortgage securities because they had been too generous in their ratings to the banks that issued these securities. How independent Moody's is of their paying customers is up for debate.

Are Moody's Ratings Reliable?

Another question that you hear raised about Moody and its ratings concerns how reliable they are. Moody's claims that it makes judgments on the future of companies and governments in order to protect investors. Because of this, they try to consider the worst possible outcomes of the entity under consideration for the foreseeable future.

This means that Moody's ratings are not only comprised of statistical factors, but also their best appraisal of risks over the long term. The ratings that Moody's provides also reflect the opinion of this investors' service on the credit worthiness of any organization and its securities. Moody's is also quick to point out that these ratings do not qualify as commercial credit ratings.

You may have heard some stinging criticisms of Moody's in the past. They were blamed for the enormous losses that investors realized in the collapse of the collateralized debt market during the financial crisis of 2007-2009.

Even though Moody's awarded the highest ratings to these CDO instruments, many of them experienced losses of from thirty to fifty percent in value at this time. Credit Suisse Group had issued over $340 million of ABS CDO's and the losses amounted to around $125 million, even though Moody's rated them as AAA.

Moody's reliability has also been questioned by the way that they treated voices of dissent within their own ranks. Executives and analysts who gave warnings about troubles in the housing market and dependent debt instruments were fired in 2007 even as the housing market began to collapse. The company was blamed by the McClatchy investigation of putting profits ahead of reliable ratings on these investments.

Other countries have accused Moody's of acts of economic terrorism. The European Union and Portugal have questioned why Moody's has encouraged speculation and attacks on Portuguese bonds in their bias towards their ratings. Public utilities in Portugal have similarly been downgraded even when they enjoyed solid streams of foreign revenues and strong financial profiles.

Who is Behind Moodys' Ratings?

You can not point fingers at any one party when you look at Moody's Ratings. They are a publicly traded company that enjoys special US government charters.

The largest stake holder is legendary billionaire investor Warren Buffet, who has owned anywhere from ten to nearly twenty percent of their stock at a time.

Would you be surprised to see Moody's downgrade Warren Buffet's Berkshire Hathaway company's ratings when this is the case?

Seven Steps to Protect Yourself From Economic Meltdown

You should know something about the economic forecasts of Robert Wiedemer the famed economist, who correctly predicted the collapse of the housing market, credit markets, jobs market, stock market, U.S. government debt, and U.S. dollar market. He has since then made further predictions for the American economy in the years 2012 and beyond.

They read much like a Mayan calendar doomsday scenario. This prescient economist claims that you will witness a fifty percent unemployment rate, a ninety percent stock market decline, and a doubling of inflation each year for three straight years as the U.S. government debt and dollar bubbles finally collapse completely.

Since Robert Wiedemer has been deadly accurate in his last several predictions of this decade, all of which he made when everyone else was caught up in the irrational exuberance, you should take his warning of a near total U.S. economic collapse the next year or the following one very seriously.

In the paragraphs that follow, you will learn what are the seven emergency steps that you can take today to protect yourself, your family, and your finances from personal economic meltdown.

Step Number 1 - If You Own a Home, Refinance or Consider Foreclosure

If you are not already in foreclosure or behind on your home's mortgage, you may question the wisdom of this first piece of advice. The fact is that you have to reduce your monthly outlays now in advance of the strong possibility that you current job simply will no longer exist within two years or less.

Downsize immediately in order to start saving as much money as you possibly can. You can take this money and pour it into physical gold and silver holdings that you keep in a safe in your home. Now that is a safe asset that you can count on no matter how badly things get in the United States.

Step Number 2 - If you Have High Amount of Personal Debt, Consider Bankruptcy

For all of you who still have a decent credit rating, you are probably raising your eyebrows. The fact of the matter is that you will never pay off a high personal debt in the amount of time that remains to you before a financial meltdown overtakes you like a giant rushing tsunami. What can you do in order to restore order to your crumbling financial house? Declare personal bankruptcy.

If you can get a Chapter Seven petition approved, this is the route that you should take. It would wipe out all personal debts, credit card bills, and car loans. With the enormous interest payments that you will save each month, you should get some non U.S. dollar denominated assets. Once again, you can not go wrong in any economic malaise when you acquire physical and tangibly held gold and silver.

Step Number 3 - Get Rid of Any Luxury Items and Cars. Downsize Your Monthly Expense

In the continuing theme of downsizing ahead of an economic disaster, you should dispose of any luxury cars and items that you really do not need. If they are paid off, then you can sell them and bank the profits in precious metals. If not, then you should eliminate any monthly payments on them so that you can save aggressively. Do not delay with this step, as by definition, you can immediately do without luxury goods, vehicles, and other items.

Step Number 4 - Get Financially Educated and Understand What is Happening in the Global Financial Market

You are in all too common company if you do not fully grasp what is going on in the world wide financial markets. The European sovereign debt crisis, U.S. potential credit downgrades and narrowly avoided debt ceiling induced defaults, and potential hard landings for China are not simply glitzy catch phrases. In fact, your personal financial future is inextricably intertwined with these concepts.

You can never go wrong when you invest your time, efforts, and resources in a sound and practical financial education. This can be obtained through any number of really good books, magazines, financial newspapers, and seminars. Robert Kiyosaki's "Rich Dad, Poor Dad," series remains the number one best seller personal help finance book of all time.

You might start there. Barron's, Forbes, the Wall Street Journal, and Fortune all produce excellent financial education magazines or newspapers that can keep you up to date on the economic trends that affect you, your family, and your finances intimately.

Step Number 5 - Share Your Resources with Neighbors and Friends

You are always well served to show kindness to your friends and neighbors. The Golden Rule "Do Unto Others as you Would Have them do unto you" is just as relevant today as it was two thousand years ago when Jesus first spoke it.

If your personal economics decline sharply in the future, you may well need the favor returned to you. Aside from creating a community safety net of sorts for yourself in the dark days that could very well lie ahead, this kindness will give you immense personal satisfaction. "It is more blessed to give than to receive" also still applies in every way that you can possibly imagine.

Step Number 6 - Protect your Retirement Account and Switch Your 401k to Hold Gold and Silver

Most of you have some form of savings for retirement. You probably keep these assets, whether they be stocks, bond, mutual funds, or Real Estate Investment Trusts, in your 401K or IRA. Both of these accounts are in jeopardy, as the government has the power to seize them and issue you worthless Treasury bonds in place of their assets whenever it suits them, or should the need arise in a dire financial catastrophe.

You can avoid this if you sell off the assets in them and take the distribution with a thirty percent penalty, and then invest the proceeds in gold and silver that you hold physically in a safe. Alternatively, you could risk the possibility of government seizure and fight against the decline of stocks, bonds, and mutual funds when you set up a Gold 401k.

This will permit you to hold several different kinds of gold and silver coins and bullion in it, such as U.S. Gold Eagles, Gold Buffaloes, and Silver dollars. As the markets decline in the event of a pending economic meltdown, your assets will only go up in value as the flight to real quality begins in earnest. There simply is not enough gold and silver to go around when the chips are down.

Step Number 7 - Create Your Own Bank

Commercial banks would not lend out money to consumers who might not have a job anymore in the aftermath of a more severe financial crisis. You can get around this by becoming your own bank. This is not so difficult as it sounds.

All that you have to do is to obtain a Whole Life Insurance Policy from a well funded and solidly founded insurance company. Make sure that it has a guaranteed annual return on it, and that it also pays dividends consistently. This will allow you to build up a significant policy value that you can borrow against interest free whenever you have financial needs.

With Citibank's scary Great Depression charts versus today's stock market charts calling for a possible collapse of the stock market in the next four to six months, what do you have to lose when you take early steps to protect your own personal financial state now?

The Real Key to Building Wealth Is Adding Economic Value

You probably realize that there are many ways to measure economic value that is added to a company. Such value is built up as all of the interest holders in a company recognize that there is a major improvement in the benefits or the quality of the firm and its products or services.

The typical means to measure a company's results include net profit margin, return on net worth, operating profit margin, profit after tax, and return on investment. Return on investment may be the most popular means to measure how a company performs today, but it is not the most effective one available. The reality is that all of these various measurements have their own limitations in the competitive marketplace of today.

A newer and more effective means to determine a company's success is called Economic Value Added. In the paragraphs below, you will learn about the Economic Value Added measurement and why this is the real key to build up wealth.

Who Invented Economic Value Added?

More than one organization has claimed to invent the idea of Economic Value Added, or EVA.

Peter Drucker argues that he detailed this EVA concept in his work "Managing for Results" that was published in 1964. While it is true that he discussed it nearly fifty years ago, it was not until Stern Steward & Co, a New York based consulting firm, fully developed the concept in 1982 that it came into popular use.

Stern Steward & Co. promoted this phrase and idea heavily to maximize corporate manager value adding behavior. The phrase appeared in "The Quest for Value" in 1991 as well. Though several organizations and individuals may have contributed to the origination and development of the Economic Value Added concept, Stern Steward & Co holds the registered trade mark on the idea. They marketed it so successfully that it became a popular concept with which businesses can measure value.

What is Economic Value Added?

The Economic Value Added formula can be determined by taking the opportunity costs of capital that is invested and subtracting this from the Net Operating Profit After Tax. To figure out the capital's opportunity cost, you simply measure the quantity of capital that is used according to the average weighed cost of Debt and Equity Capital. This gives you a reliable measurement for the economic profit.

There are various definitions for Economic Value Added. The easiest way to explain it is as the monetary value of a firm at the conclusion of a given time frame less the monetary value of the identical firm at the commencement of the time frame. It is also an economic profit estimate that companies can use.

As such, this EVA value represents a complete measurement for a company's operating performance. It allows you to determine the change of a business' financial worth on a year by year basis. This tool is more effective than just net income since it factors in the cost of all capital that is employed to create the income.

Joel Stern, the long time CEO of Stern Steward & Co., describes Economic Value Added as a means to leverage a firm's greatest asset. This is not just its capital, but is especially its unique assets that include the energy, creativity, and talent of its employees. This is how firms are able to optimize their wealth creation and the reason that the Economic Value Added measurement and process is so potent.

How Is Economic Value Added Different from Other Economic Measurements?

Obviously there are several other popular measuring sticks in use today for how a business performs. You have already seen that Return on Investment Capital is among the most popular ones. Earnings Before Income, Taxes, Depreciation, and Amortization and Earnings Per Share are two other widely used tools in business circles nowadays. EVA is distinct from these three measurements as it includes all of the various costs to run a company. This includes financial and operating costs.

What Does Economic Value Added Allow?

The real benefit that you see when you use EVA is that you are able to put funds to work in the activities where the Net Operating Profit After Taxes is higher than the actual capital's cost.

If you have business operations where this Net Operating Profit After Taxes is lower than the capital's cost, it allows you to prudently remove funds from these activities.

This permits you to increase the business' operating efficiency. It also allows you to maintain the same amount of Net Operating Profit After Taxes even when you use less capital, or to grow your Net Operating Profit After Taxes with the same amount of capital. Think what you could do with additional capital.

This means when you use Economic Value Added that you are able to invest in the most important projects and activities that will ultimately enhance the wealth of the corporate shareholders. This activity will cause the value of the stock to rise as well, and will help the company's market value to increase.

It is still possible that activities which do not grow the value of the shareholder might be in the interests of the stakeholders. Social responsibility and customer satisfaction are also important non monetary ideals. A technology might be more expensive than the value it creates, and yet ensure that the environment is not polluted by the manufacturing process, as one example.

What Are the 4 "M" Applications of Economic Value Added?

Stern Steward says that you can sum up the four best applications of EVA with four words that start with the first letter "M." The first of these words is measurement. It is now widely accepted that Economic Value Added proves to be the most correct measurement for how a corporation performs during any set time frame. This is despite the fact that there are other popular measuring tools for performance like Return on Investment and Per Share Earnings.

EVA also helps to instill the proper mindset in employees and managers. Financial management and compensation by Economic Value Added radically change a company's culture. EVA places all operations and financial activities on an equal footing. This gives the various employees of a corporation a true language of communication in common.

The proper mindset is encouraged by effective motivation. Employees can realize the longer term perspectives of a business owner as well as their inherent feelings of the importance and urgency of a task or project when they are properly motivated. Stern Stewart accomplishes this by putting into place cash based bonus plans. This encourages the managers to behave as if they owned the company, since they are paid in much the same way as the company's owners are.

Finally, you see an effective management system established through Economic Value Added policies. When this is designed to include all procedures, policies, processes, measurements, and methods which guide both the overall strategy and daily operations, then a company's best value can be achieved.

Economic Value Added systems take into account all decisions that management makes. This involves the allocation of capital, strategic planning practices, divestiture and acquisition price determination, daily operating decisions, and the creation and implementation of yearly goals.

Can you think of a better way to maximize a company's full value than this?

The Book of Revelation Predicts A New Economic Disorder

There is no shortage of books that you have seen published on the subject of the economic malaise and instability that continue to plague the world since the financial crisis and Great Recession broke out back in 2007.

You will find that many of these types of books point fingers and take names on who is responsible for the collapse that everyone has felt touch their lives and those of their families, neighbors, and friends in some personal way.

One such work, "The New Economic Disorder" by Dr. Larry Bates, does something different than to simply assign blame. In the paragraphs below, you will learn what this interesting work says about the financial meltdown and how it may have been predicted in the Bible book of Revelation thousands of years ago.

Who Is the Author Dr. Larry Bates?

You will find that author Dr. Larry Bates has some impressive credentials to his name. He is the editor, publisher, and economist for the "Monetary and Economic Review." He has served in the Tennessee State House of Representatives in the past as its Committee on Banking and Commerce chairman. Besides this, Dr. Bates had a successful career as the CEO of a bank.

He has been a professor of banking and money for the Tennessee State College System and the Bank Administration Institute as well. Larry Bates is furthermore a well recognized international speaker on the topics of the Federal Reserve and political systems and the ways that these impact both your finances specifically and the economy as a whole. He also currently serves as the Chief Executive Officer of IRN USA Radio News and the Information Radio Network. Because of all of these numerous credential to his name, you should give him serious consideration.

What is the Premise of "The New Economic Disorder?"

Dr. Larry Bates throws down the gauntlet hard in the premise of "The New Economic Disorder" when he boldly declares that he believes the financial meltdown was foretold by the Bible thousands of years ago. He takes you through the devastating and all too familiar events of the last few years in a true expose of how this happened.

You can not argue with his back story claims that America still struggles with the ongoing financial crisis. He reminds you that unemployment continues to remain incredibly high, homes still fall into foreclosure at near record rates, and the real costs of living only continue to rise by the day.

What did the Bible have to say about these days that test your mettle and resolve? The Bible talks about a terrible crisis in the world that leads to the rise of a one world order and central world government. Bates walks you through the events that continue to unfold and to force the nations of the world into ever closer cooperation and central governance.

He argues that the worst is still to come. According to Dr. Bates, there will be a total economic and financial collapse so profound that the world leaders will have no choice but to pool their sovereignty and resources together into a single world wide effort in order to effectively combat the unprecedented global economic crisis and to restore order to the world.

What Topics Are Covered in "The New Economic Disorder?"

You will see some very interesting and pertinent topics covered in Dr. Larry Bates' "The New Economic Disorder." The writer comprehends and internalizes the vast challenges and structural problems that face the U.S. and Western economies.

He lays out a series of five potent, perilous, and indomitable forces that continue to create the intractable economic problems. Among these are your disappearing financial privacy, continuous and increased government manipulation of the economy that creates a false sense of prosperity, the debt bubble and its impact on your personal investments, and the rise of the new world order.

Where your investments are concerned, "The New Economic Disorder" covers many different areas. These include stocks, mutual funds, bonds, real estate, insurance, and bank accounts and banking in general. Dr. Bates does more than simply show you the problems that continue to afflict the economy.

He goes beyond the ways that these have influenced and will continue to impact your personal investments. What sets his work apart from the other dozens in the same genre on the book store shelves is that he is all at once confident, truthful, and crystal clear in his proposed solutions to the struggles the economy faces.

For Larry Bates, this answer is the Bible, where he states that you can find a real and permanent cure for the economic virus that only seems to grow worse with each day.

What Has Changed in the Revised and Updated Edition?

Since 2001 when the first edition of Dr. Bates' "The New Economic Disorder" hit the shelves, you have witnessed many of the what might have seemed at the time to be outlandish conspiracy plots that he outlined actually come to pass. He predicted a financial crisis on a scale never before seen.

In his newer 2009 revised and updated version of the provocative and compelling work, he includes a great deal of new information on what caused the mortgage crisis, the problems with America and the Western world's personal debt loads that are rising exponentially, your own personal investments and how you should carefully proceed with them in the coming difficult economic years, and many other pertinent topics that you have seen take the center stage of the economic world.

What Is the Final Verdict of "The New Economic Disorder?"

The bad news is that Dr. Bates only forecasts more hard times to come for the U.S. and the West and these nations' citizens like yourself. The better news is that Dr. Bates cheerfully demonstrates to you that despite the financial tsunami that the Bible saw coming and prophesied literally thousands of yeas ago, there is still both time and hope for you to order your financial house before the really traumatic collapse overwhelms you, your family, and your friends.

"The New Economic Disorder" is not light bed time reading, nor is it for you who are faint of heart. If you can put aside your personal biases and fears and approach the interesting book with a clear and open mind, then it just might save you from the dark economic waters that seem to surround you at every turn any more.

The book does present the economic problems in a clear and simple to grasp manner. It goes through the serious problems that wrack the national and world economies and how they relate to you personally. If you take the author's advice, and he continues to be right with his predictions of economic doom and gloom, then you can hope for not only your own survival in these difficult days, but also in your ability to thrive and prosper while the masses look in vain for solutions and hope.

Dr. Bates finds his answers in the Judeo-Christian God of the Bible, whom he confidently believes has everything in hand and has a master plan through all of this mess. Whether you choose to agree with him or not, you should consider and keep in mind that tens of millions of Americans take his point of view very seriously indeed.

When you read this book you will walk away with one question that either haunts you or personally challenges and inspires you, and this depends on both your personal outlook on life and your own religious and spiritual world view. Will you survive the new economic disorder?

<u>POLITICS</u>

"Banking and Government Interventions"

Politics

Silver Will Skyrocket When The Leasing Scam is Revealed

When you think about silver prices, you probably do not realize that there is a manipulation that goes on every day that has held them artificially low. This phenomenon is called the silver leasing scam.

After years of turning a blind eye to it, the Commodities and Futures Trading Commission has finally opened an exhaustive investigation into the practice. The effects of this investigation are wide ranging and could dramatically impact the market prices for silver in the near to medium term future.

In the paragraphs that follow, you will learn what is involved with silver leasing, who is behind the unethical practice, and how it will cause the prices to skyrocket when the scam is banned.

What is the Purpose of Leasing Silver?

The first question that should come to your mind is why would someone want to lease out their silver in the first place? The mega banks hold enormous inventories of silver and gold to back up their financial institutions and reassure depositors and customers that they are stable.

These precious metals preserve the long term wealth of the bank quite well. The problem that these bullion banks have with their large holdings is that they do not generate any wealth when they sit in the vaults and collect dust.

Greed entered the picture as the big bullion banks looked for a way to earn some revenue from these silver and gold holdings. They did not want to actually sell their precious silver stockpiles, but only to find a way to earn income on them while they are on the balance sheet.

The answer to this dilemma that the bullion banks faced was to lease out the metals. If they could just find some smaller banks to loan the metals to at the rate of one to two percent of the actual silver metal value each year, then they would be able to realize revenues and profits while they still maintained a legal ownership of the precious metals.

How Can Silver be Leased?

It is easy to see how the major banks were able to lease out their silver, once they found willing customers. They would simply sign a contract for a period of time and interest rate. Then they would deliver the physical silver to a customer with the under-standing that they did not have to receive the exact same silver back.

This is what makes silver leasing possible. So long as they get the exact weight of silver bars back at the end of their lease, the major institution that owns the silver is perfectly happy.

The willing customers that the mega banks found to lease their silver to turned out to be smaller banks that also had an idea to make money from the silver lease.

These small banks were willing to pay a one to two percent fee for the use of the precious metals because they would turn around and sell this silver on the open market.

They could then take the money that they received and invest it into stable assets with a higher yield of three to four percent, such as Treasuries or other safe investments. This gave them the income to pay their lease fees and still make a percent or two for themselves.

How Does this Silver Leasing Affect the Price Right Now?

The main problem with silver leasing is that it creates a false scenario in the market. Most banks that do these leases never intend to return the metal. They just keep rolling their lease contracts over with the large bullion banks.

Since the small banks that lease the silver from the silver owning banks turn around and sell the metal without any plans to repurchase and return it, it makes it look like there is far more silver on the world market than there really is.

The additional supply that has been sold does not really exist, since it has been borrowed. Although the supply is a lie and unreal, the depressing effect that it has on the prices is very real. An appearance of too much supply serves to keep the prices of silver artificially low.

Who is Behind the Leasing Scam?

By this point, you probably wonder who could be involved in such unscrupulous activity as to loan out silver that they never intend to repatriate while they still show it on their balance sheet as inventory on hand.

The Commodities and Futures Trading Commission's ongoing investigation has helped to make it possible to name culprits and point fingers of blame. JP Morgan is considered to be one of the worst offenders for leasing out silver, but it is not alone. Goldman Sachs, HSBC, AIG, and the Bank of Nova Scotia are others whose names are on the list of habitual offenders.

What Will Happen When this Scam is Finally Fully Exposed or Even Restricted or Forbidden?

Since an investigation is already underway, the silver leasing scam is currently in the process of being exposed. You can see what has happened to silver prices in the meanwhile. They have rocketed up from under $20 per ounce to over $35 per ounce on simple conjecture that this practice will be broken up.

The longer term ramifications of the end of the silver lease practice are far greater than this. Should the point come where the activity is declared illegal and broken up, the banks that borrowed the silver do not have it and will not be able to return it. This is especially a problem because there is so little inventory of physical silver available for them to buy and return.

In fact, there is an insufficient quantity of silver above ground for them to make good on their borrowed silver commitments. To put it in perspective, an entire two years of silver production has been loaned out and sold for such industrial applications as medical products, electrical and computer goods, solar panels, military hardware, photography, and literally thousands of other applications.

This silver has been used up and can not be recovered. Meanwhile, there is not even an entire year's worth of silver supply available above ground to be purchased. You can see that silver prices would have to go far higher in order for the borrowing banks to have any hope at all of returning their sliver lease metals. On top of this, it is easily possible that they simply would not be able to obtain this quantity of silver today at any price.

Besides potentially much higher silver prices and even silver shortages, there will likely be legal consequences when silver leasing is prohibited. There is already speculation that the firms from JP Morgan and Goldman Sachs to AIG and Bank of Nova Scotia that have engaged in it will be held liable and charged enormous civil and regulatory penalties, since they will have been found guilty of silver manipulation that went on for over fifteen years.

It is highly possible that the principals at these companies who made the decisions to lease out the silver illegally will also face criminal prosecution and even substantial time in prison.

Can you see silver prices going lower when the silver leasing scam is about to be blown wide open?

Become Your Own Bank - The Infinite Banking Concept

Have you ever realized how much interest you pay to banks when you buy a car or a house? The sad truth is that you as an average American spend in excess of thirty-four percent of all your after tax dollars per year on interest over the course of your life between mortgages on houses, car payments, and credit card bills.

There is a way to get around this interest trap that costs you more than a million dollars over the course of your life. You can do it when you became your own bank and use a concept known as infinite banking. In the paragraphs below, you will see how it is that the wealthy always get wealthier, how you can borrow from yourself like they do, and what the miracle of compound interest is really all about.

How the Wealthy Get Wealthier Automatically

It is more than just a casual observation that the wealthy are always growing richer. Experts say that if you took all of the money in the world and evenly redistributed it to everyone on the planet, in only ten years' time, ninety-seven percent of all of the money on earth would be back in the hands of only three percent of the people.

The reason that this is true is because of banking and the banking equation. While you spend over a third of your income after taxes on interest, you only save five percent of your income on average. The wealthy know how to use banking to their advantage so that they profit tremendously and do not have to pay this enormous amount of money for interest. Instead, the rich use money that you and others pay as interest and put it into investments that provide cash flow, passive income, or money that you do not have to work to get, and better real interest rates.

The Principle of Borrowing on Your Own

The problem that you have is that you lack access to funds that you can use for free or little interest like the rich do. There is a way to overcome this so that you can keep a much greater portion of your income in the future. It happens when you become your own bank, so that you can cut out the interest and profit of the middle man traditional lenders. How can you set up your own bank? You do this when you utilize the vehicle of a permanent life insurance policy.

You may already know that with permanent life insurance, you are able to borrow money from such a whole life policy. This is what sets it apart from a term insurance policy, where you only pay for life insurance coverage for a certain period of time. The problem that you run into with most whole life policies that prevents you from borrowing from them is that you do not pay high enough premiums to build up the value of this policy.

Lower premiums leave you with a lesser amount of money that you can tap to finance major purchases in your life.

If you instead select a life insurance policy with higher premiums, or one that allows you to make larger premiums than are due, then you can rapidly build up a substantial value.

This will allow you to gain enough equity value in your policy over four years time frame so that can borrow the money from the policy to buy a new car. Since there is no interest payment attached to money that you borrow from your whole insurance policy, you will not lose the huge amount of cash flow and income that interest typically consumes.

The importance of this concept can not be overlooked. When you build up your own bank through a whole life insurance policy that pays dividends, you will not have to pay either interest or taxes on the money that you borrow. Besides this, you will gain several percentage points in dividends on these premium each and every year.

This will allow you to handle your major finance needs in your life time, as well as to build up a substantial amount of life insurance for your family. Most importantly, you will not have to bleed out the huge amount of money that you otherwise pay in interest charges to finance companies and banks when you acquire things that you need like houses, cars, business equipment, education costs, big appliances, or even investment opportunities.

The Effect of Compounding Interest Over Time

You gain other advantages that the wealthy employ when you set up your own bank through an infinite banking concept. Money that you save in such a whole life insurance policy plan grows at a compound interest, not only simple interest.

Compound interest has been called the eighth wonder of the world, as well as a miracle that you can use to grow your wealth over time.

The difference between simple and compound interest is easy to understand but it is profound. Simple interest will only pay you money on your principal. Compound interest actually pays interest on both your principal and on the interest that you have already earned. There are also different ways that interest can be compounded, or added on to your account, as well. When interest compounds more frequently, this leads to greater earnings and higher principal over time.

Compound interest works out to be an incredibly potent part of your personal bank since the interest tacks on to your principal and then itself gets counted in the next interest period. This means that the interest or dividends that you earn apply to this greater balance. With compound interest, your account will grow so much faster than with only simple interest.

The best part about compound interest with whole life insurance policy dividends is that these dividends that you receive at a compounded rate come to you tax free up to the point that you withdraw instead of borrowing the money. Every year, the amount of interest and dividends that your account earns will be higher than the one before, since your account grows at a tax free compounded interest rate.

Examples of Growing Money over Time

Look at an example of ten thousand dollars that you build up in a whole life insurance policy as a personal bank.

If you only receive simple interest at five percent, then each year you would be given five hundred dollars in interest. Over a ten year period, such an account would grow to fifteen thousand dollars in value.

If instead your interest compounded once per year, the same ten thousand dollars would grow to $16,289. With most banks and insurance policies, you can receive interest that is compounded quarterly. This makes a bigger difference over time. In ten years, the money will grow to $16,436. If you set up your own bank in a vehicle that compounds monthly, you will receive a higher $16,470.

Now stretch these dollar amounts over a longer amount of time to really see what a difference compound interest can make. Ten thousand dollars becomes twenty thousand dollars in twenty years with only simple interest. The annual compound rate grows your account to $26,533. At a quarterly rate, the ten thousand becomes $27,015, while at a monthly rate it increases to $27,126.

Is it any wonder the rich grow their money so much faster than you since they use compound interest and borrow against their own assets instead of paying interest?

More information about Infinite Banking:
www.infinitebanking.org

Will Two More Years of Low Interest Rates Help the US?

You can not have missed the barrage of bad economic news lately. On any financial channel, major newspaper front page, or radio talk show, they discuss how the economy looks like it will careen towards another recession.

The Federal Reserve is the institution in the United States that seeks to carry out a dual mandate of low unemployment and economic growth along with low rates of inflation. They have recently issued another update on the economy that speaks volumes about where the country is and where it is headed over the next several years.

What Does the Latest Fed Statement Say?

On August 9th, the Federal Reserve Open Market Committee, or FOMC, issued their latest statement on the U.S. economy. They said that the data they have obtained and analyzed in June demonstrated to them that the United States' economic growth has turned out to be significantly slower than what they anticipated in past meetings.

Their leading indicators that they consider showed you that the labor market has continued to deteriorate, which contributes to the higher unemployment rate of 9.2% that you have seen emerge recently.

They also learned that the consumer spending that accounts for at least two thirds of the U.S. economy has flattened out. Purchases of commercial and industrial buildings remain weak. As if this were not enough, the housing market continues to hover in a state of perpetual depression.

The FOMC committee expanded their analysis after they came to this sobering conclusion. They announced that the recovery will go on at a slower rate than they believed it would at their previous meeting. They have revised their outlook for the unemployment rate, and now believe that it will only slowly return to levels that they consider to be acceptable and normal. They also stated that the potential downside to the economy is now greater than before.

The Fed stated that they would maintain their target federal funds interest rate levels in the range of from zero to a quarter of a percentage point. They believe that the real economic conditions will support a low level of interest rates for the foreseeable future.

They said that they are not worried about inflation because they believe that resources in the U.S. will continue to be utilized at a lower than normal rate. The biggest announcement from the Fed was that they intend to keep the federal funds national interest rates at the extremely low levels of today until at least the middle of 2013.

What Does the Latest Fed Statement Mean?

This is an important statement from the FOMC, but what does it mean for the economy and for you personally?

For starters, you can already feel in your gut that the U.S. economic recovery has slowed way down.

There is now serious debate over whether there will be stagnant U.S. economic growth for the next few years, or even potentially outright recession. The Fed sells it softer than this in their statement in order to keep markets and individuals calm, but that is the economic reality on the ground that both the analysts and economists talk about and fear.

Because of their very legitimate fears that the economy will tip back into recession, the Fed has announced that it will not begin to tighten up interest rates. In fact, they have actually given out an earliest date for when they will raise the interest rates. This is no sooner than the middle of 2013.

The Fed is known to play down expectations. They have done so as they kept incredibly low interest rates since the Great Recession forced them to aggressively cut said rates from four percent and higher down to practically zero. It is very conceivable that it will be the year 2014 or even later before they actually feel comfortable enough to raise the national interest rates, which will summarily curtail economic growth.

The last vestiges of the Federal Reserve's famous failure Quantitative Easing 2 are the securities that they continue to hold. They have decided as the principal payments come back in on these Treasuries, as well as collateralized loans that they bought from bank balance sheets that were in serious trouble, they will continue to use them to buy up more Treasuries.

The reason that they do this is because as there are more buyers of government bonds, the price of these Treasuries goes up. Since interest rates on bonds move inversely to the price, as the Fed drives the prices up with their asset purchase reinvestment program, they help to hold down the de facto interest rates that affect the cars, houses, and other large ticket items that you buy on credit.

How Do Low Interest Rates Cause Monetary Expansion?

When there are lower interest rates over a sustained period of time, such as you have seen since 2009, there are other consequences. Banks are able to expand the national money supply as they make additional loans to businesses and consumers at lower, more attractive interest rates. They do this through the fractional reserve banking system, the little known and understood way that U.S. and practically all banking systems on earth operate today.

This means that as the Fed pumps more money into the banking system with its asset purchases, and as interest rates are extremely low, then banks have more money that they are allowed to loan out because they are only required to keep around a 10% fraction of their reserves on hand. They can loan out the rest. The net result is a stealth increase of the national money supply of U.S. dollars.

What Will Happen to Inflation Rates As the Money Supply Expands?

Now you have more money that the Fed will indirectly but deliberately create in order to stimulate the economy.

You probably have heard the time tested adage that Milton Friedman argued which states that inflation results from more money that chases the same quantity of goods and services.

The undesired side effects will be higher inflation rates, since the number of goods and services produced in the United States has not risen appreciably since 2007. In this time, the Federal Reserve has more than tripled the amount of U.S. dollars in circulation.

Higher inflation is the double edge to the two edged sword of the dangerous game that "Helicopter" Ben Bernake and his Federal Reserve open market committee play on a daily basis. He earned this nickname from a speech that he made when he famously said that if you gave him a large enough helicopter filled with money, then he could fly around the nation and throw the cash out to the cheering masses below in order to save the U.S. economy from slowdown, recession, and even depression. That is what you call an expansion of the money supply.

Why Has Gold Gone Higher While Silver Does not Move?

Higher inflation expectations cause investors to pile into the precious metals, especially gold. This is because gold is correctly perceived to be the time tested best shelter for your money in times of higher inflation and all around uncertainty in the world. Gold has played this sacred role all throughout recorded history.

Silver historically served a similar function. The gray metal today has more factors that influence it than gold does. Silver is very much an industrial metal with 10,000 different applications and uses.

Besides this, the Chicago Mercantile Exchange has repeatedly attacked leveraged silver positions when they raised the margin requirements to control silver positions a dozen times in only a few months. This has helped to hold the silver prices down while gold has outperformed.

When the chips are down economically and you need a safe place to lodge your paper money, can you think of a better safe haven than the two precious metals that have protected the wealth of mankind for over five thousand years?

The CPI Consumer Price Index - Manipulated And Obsolete

Whenever you go to the store, you can feel the higher prices practically all of the time. You have probably wondered why more is not made of this in official government statistics.

There is an index that is supposed to measure the changes in prices for things that you need to live, such as clothes, food, gasoline, and housing.

This index is called the CPI, or Consumer Price Index. In the paragraphs that follow, you will see exactly what this index is, how it is figured, why it matters, and the reason that today's version of it does not reflect the reality that you see on the ground.

What is the CPI Consumer Price Index?

You should know that the Bureau of Labor Statistics, or the BLS, defines the Consumer Price Index as the change in prices that urban individuals pay to buy a sample basket of both consumer products and services.

The BLS develops this information every month based on variations in prices that consumers in these urban areas experience.

This estimate is put together with a collection of tens of thousands of items whose prices are tracked over time. This data is intended to record changes in the costs of services and products that American households purchase.

The CPI's history dates back to the mid 1880's. In these years, the Bureau of Labor received a request from Congress to determine the effects that new tariffs were having on prices. Around thirty years later, these statistics were formulated into a measurement that looked something like the CPI today. It was utilized to determine how much shipbuilders' wages should go up in World War I.

These types of inflation stats were routinely published from 1921 on and became widely accepted and utilized following World War II. At this point, Union contracts began to rely on this data for adjustments in wages based on changes to the cost of living.

How is the CPI calculated?

The BLS gathers an enormous amount of information to calculate this Consumer Price Index. They start out with calls and visits to literally thousands of rental units, stores, service outlets, and even doctor's office around the country. This allows them to record the costs of some eighty thousand different items every month. They do not select these items randomly, but choose them scientifically to represent the items that consumers typically buy.

Once this information is recorded, it is then dispatched to the Bureau of Labor Statistics national office. Commodity experts in specific areas look over the information to make sure that it is both consistent with the prior months' data and accurate.

They adjust the data as the feel is necessary based on changes in the quantity in a packaged up good or alterations to quality or features of the item.

They then average these items together according to an assigned weighting for each component. Housing is counted at over forty-one percent. Beverages and food weigh in at over seventeen percent. Transportation costs factor in at seventeen percent. Medical care is assigned around seven percent. Clothing counts for six percent and entertainment for around four and a half percent. The other items category is about seven percent. The BLS never considers taxes as a factor in the cost of living, even though they are a significant part of many family's expenses.

What is the CPI's Purpose?

Originally, the CPI was created to offer people, businesses, and government knowledge of the costs of inflation. All of these groups need to be aware of how much less their money will purchase in the future. Since its early years, the CPI has grown into something much more significant.

The Consumer Price Index is actually quite important for a number of people today. The government utilizes this change in percentage each year to gauge inflation, or higher costs of goods and services. As such, this CPI is employed to index many workers' salaries and retiree's pensions. For example, the entire social security retirement program, with its fifty million recipients, is set up with cost of living increases that are based on changes to the CPI.

Millions of American workers receive wage increases based on the CPI increase too. Retirees from Federal Civil and Military service all receive cost of living increases pegged to the CPI number as well. For welfare beneficiaries like those who get food stamps or free lunches at school, their benefits are influenced by CPI changes. Unions still adjust their collective bargaining for wage increases based on changes to the CPI.

What Government Interference has Rendered the CPI Obsolete?

Until the early 1980's, the CPI did its job fairly well. Over the last few decades though, the BLS has gradually given in to intense pressure from politicians who were eager to portray inflation as lower than it has actually been. There were several ways that they accomplished this.

The BLS began to allow for greater flexibility in what they called substitutions. They would allow for consumers to substitute hamburgers as the equivalent of a steak. Besides this, they more subtly accounted for this new substitution formula by altering the weighting of different goods that were counted in the fixed CPI basket.

During the Clinton years, the BLS phased out the more honest arithmetic factoring of items in the CPI in favor of a new geometric weighting. Under the geometric form of weight assignments, they counted CPI items whose prices were going up at a lower weight, while they similarly assigned a higher weight to components whose prices declined.

How much of a difference did this make? Geometric weighting lowered the yearly change of the CPI by 2.7%.

When this amount is compounded from the early 1990's, the impact on CPI has been so dramatic that the social security cost of living increases are over a third lower than what they should have been using the original weighting methods.

When an enhancement is made to a product or service, then the BLS discounts increases to the prices of the item year over year. A newer washing machine with electronic features might actually cost twenty percent more than last year's older push button model. The BLS will not account for this as rising prices, since the quality of the product is now better.

One of the greatest interferences that the BLS performs on the CPI is what they call seasonal adjustments. Commodities that are considered to be volatile, like food and energy, are toned down as they go up because of supposedly seasonal factors. Their eventual decline is fully factored in later though, which gives a downward bias to the CPI.

How much of a difference does all of this make? When all of the changes to the CPI computations are combined, John Williams of Shadow Stats says that the CPI is under reported by as much as seven percentage points. Imagine how high the official inflation numbers would be if these seven points were added in to today's two to three percent.

How would a Real CPI Index look?

A real CPI index would not try to strip out the so called volatile factors like food and energy. It would also use the same computations that were employed until the Regan and Clinton Era changes began.

Most of all, it would be consistent in counting the same items, their weightings, and their price changes from one month to the next.

After all, how many people do you know who do not purchase food or energy on a regular basis?

The Government's Dirty Secret About the Debt Crisis

News of the imminent government shut down has even reached reached the status of water cooler conversation at the office. The effects on the average American's psyche are devastating already. According to recent shocking polls taken, nearly one in two Americans now believes that the country will enter a second Great Depression next year or in 2013.

Half of Americans believe that the greatest days of the nation economically are behind us, while forty percent believe that their children's future will be less good than their own. You may not know what the painful and widespread effects of such a shutdown will be when you wake up on August third if Congress can not do something to get the debt ceiling raised by August second.

You probably are totally unaware of what the long term ramifications of the government shrinking down drastically in size will be. In the paragraphs that follow, you will learn what will happen if the debt ceiling is never raised, a truth that the government is desperate to keep from you.

Immediate Results of a Government Partial Shutdown on August 3rd

No one is one hundred percent certain what the government will do on August third if the debt ceiling has not been raised. Here are the facts that you need to know.

Since the government borrows forty-five cents of ever dollar that it actually spends, on that infamous date, the government will simply have to stop paying about forty-five percent of all of its obligations for August.

Treasury Secretary Timothy Geithner and President Barack Obama call this a catastrophe in the making. Chairman of the Federal Reserve Ben Bernake calls this calamitous. The Bipartisan Policy Center created by Congress says that this will spell major trouble for the nation's economy.

What will the immediate effects of the expenses shortfall be? Who will you see not get compensated by the Federal government if the debt ceiling is not raised? First of all, the government will make sure that the debt holders of the $14.3 Trillion in U.S. Treasuries receive their interest payments. They will also send out the Social Security checks to the retirees, mostly because they have no choice. To neglect either of these duties would be deemed either a total or technical default by the three ratings agencies Moody's, S&P, and Fitch.

This brings you back to the uncomfortable question of who will not be paid on August third. If you expect an IRS Federal income tax refund, you can anticipate that to be put on hiatus. Those of you who are among the legions of Federal Employees, such as post office workers, soldiers, and others, would probably not receive your salaries or benefits.

Veterans hospitals might be shut down temporarily. If you work for a defense vendor who counts on some of the $32 billion in payments that are due to defense contractors in August, then you may be in trouble. There is real speculation that defense industry stocks would plunge by fifty percent within hours of the announcement.

You can not argue that such actions would have terrible consequences for real people, who are not simply numbers and names in a database. For a long time, this would cause grief and anguish for many individuals who count on these paychecks, such as our devoted and sacrificing military families. Widespread economic hardship could multiply if the stock market tanked and the economy tipped back into recession as a result of this temporary default. It would not be the financial end of the U.S., but it would cause economic chaos that might last a long, long time.

What Are the Real Long Term Ramifications of Such A Shutdown?

Now you know the worst of the news. But there is another side of the equation that is completely ignored by the financial media and news talking heads. Should the government be unable to agree on a debt ceiling increase over the long term, there is a result that few expect and the government does not want you to know about at all. This is that after the effects of the very real hardship had lessened, you would see a United States emerge that was potentially stronger, richer, better off, and certainly less cocky than in the past.

This does not mean that you would pay less in taxes. On the contrary, the government has insufficient revenue for its size today as things currently stand. What you would see is far less government. This means that there would be substantially less government interference in the economy. You would not have so many government employee eaters, but would instead see more private sector contributors emerge as a result. You would have more license to build wealth and expand existing businesses or to open new ones. This additional freedom could start an economic revolution not seen since the bygone days of beloved President Reagan.

This would happen for two reasons. There would be more creative minds put to work since they no longer had government jobs to laze around at all day. You would also see far less government regulation and interference in the ability of people to create wealth. The number of people who sit behind government desks and interfere in the businesses of hard working Americans would drop dramatically. This means that much more wealth could be created, as there were fewer people hell bent on destroying it.

The Real Reason the Federal Government Will Raise the Debt Ceiling

The odds are great that the government will come together in a rare display of bi-partisan ship. It has nothing to do with nobility, but everything to do with what the American people would learn if the government went into a partial shut down. This is that the government is the dilemma, not the answer to the problem.

In fact, you would be significantly better off if there were far less of it. This is the real reason that President Obama and his henchmen all want you to fear and dread the potential financial Armageddon that could be unleashed if they do not raise the debt ceiling. It is simply because they wish to scare you and the Republicans into action before it becomes "too late."

The real "too late" at stake here is for them and their monstrous government, not for the long term national economy. You may fear like most Americans that you could not get by without the massive and bloated Federal government of today. It is simply not the case that you would starve to death without them. Instead, you would see a far more dynamic, productive, and rich society result.

After the pain and adjustment period ended, you would witness this scenario unfold right in front of you, if the government simply shrank by forty-five percent.

The U.S. economy never struggles because there is too little government regulation and interference. Instead, it suffers because there is far too much government meddling in the free enterprise system. The answer to an over abundance of government interference is not more government interference. It is a smaller government. Come August third, this is what you will begin to see if the fighting parties in Washington D.C. can not get their proverbial acts together.

Once the pain and adjustment of the lost jobs subside, does this smaller government that lives within its means really sound like such a frightening, catastrophic, and calamitous outcome to you?

The Past And Present Story of the United States Debt

Now that the debt ceiling has been raised once again, it is a good time to consider the past and present story of the United States debt. You might be surprised to learn that at no time in the two hundred and thirty five year history of this nation has the government ever held a greater literal amount of debt or a higher debt to GDP, or Gross Domestic Product, than it does today.

In the paragraphs that follow, you will come to understand how the nation's debt situation spiraled out of control to the point that America's much envied AAA sterling credit rating is now in real danger of being downgraded by Standard and Poor's Ratings agency, as well as how you can profit in this situation.

What Are the Historic Debt Levels of the U.S.?

It should not come as much of a surprise to you that the greatest debtor nation in the history of the world has usually owed public debts, even since the founding father's first set up the grandest experiment in human democracy. By the end of the war for independence, these debts were already considerable. As of January 1, 1791, the nation reported its first published debt value of just under seventy-five and a half million dollars, a not inconsiderable sum for a brand new nation at the end of the eighteenth century. War was the catalyst for the debt.

The government managed to run national budget surpluses in all but two of the following budget years until the War of 1812 broke out against the British Empire. This war grew the government debt to a greater level than the young nation had to that point experienced. Thanks to the eighteen budget surpluses in the following twenty years, the growing nation managed to pay off 99.97% of all debt owed. This was the last time the nation could achieve this impressive financial feat.

The country then tightly controlled its finances until the advent of the Civil War. The debt in 1860 stood at a mere sixty-five million dollars. In the third year of this devastating war, the debt had exceeded one billion dollars for the first time in U.S. history.

This milestone became a distant memory by 1866, as the debt had climbed to $2.7 billion after the conclusion of the Civil War. The country went back to fiscal responsibility for the next almost fifty years with thirty-six budget surplus years and only eleven deficits. Around the turn of the twentieth century, the government had paid down fifty-five percent of all the debt.

The first forty years of the twentieth century presented new financing challenges to the U.S. monetary authorities. World War I racked up a national debt bill of twenty-five and a half billion dollars, or 29.2% of GDP, by the time America had helped to win it. Still, the government managed to run eleven budget surpluses in a row afterward, and it paid down the debt by thirty-six percent.

The Great Depression unleashed Franklin D. Roosevelt's inherent love to spend as he struggled to lift the U.S. economy from the largest economic downturn this country has witnessed yet. Roosevelt assumed the presidency in 1933. In 1930 the debt stood at $16.19 billion, or 16.6% of the country's GDP.

Thanks to his significant annual deficits that ranged from two to five percent of GDP, by 1940 this amount had grown to $42.97 billion, at almost fifty percent of the national economic output in a year.

World War II increased this amount astronomically as well. Debt against GDP stood at in excess of one hundred percent by the end of this second world war. The government endeavored to run some surpluses in the post war years. This helped it to see the debt to GDP level reduced to around 93% at $257.3 billion by 1950.

In the Korean War and Vietnam years, the nation again grew the size of the debt exponentially. The debt levels roared along at the levels of inflation. From 1950 to 1980, the debt tripled in size from about $260 billion to $909 billion in 1980. Ironically, as a percentage of debt to GDP, this actually declined during this period to around thirty-three percent. That resulted from a significant period of economic growth that took place in the fifties and sixties.

When Did the Debt Situation Begin to Run Out of Control in the United States?

Presidents Reagan and the first Bush quadrupled the debt in the years from 1980 to 1992. The literal numbers of debt dollars owed advanced so rapidly that debt to GDP began to climb again. The Cold War caused this increase in percentages. By the end of the 1980's, the ratio had risen to 41% of total GDP with a debt of $3.2 trillion in 1990.

The last years that you saw the debt still under control in this country were under President Clinton. From the years 1992 to 2000, the debt rose from $3.2 trillion to $5.7 trillion by 2000. That represented a consistent 56% to 57% debt to GDP ratio.

Both republican President George W. Bush and democratic President Barrack Hussein Obama lost control of the U.S. debt levels. Under the two terms of the second President Bush, the deficit ran from $5.7 trillion to $10.7 trillion, where it reached nearly seventy percent in debt to GDP. In only two and a half years of Presdent Obama, the debt has soared at an unparalleled rate in the history of the nation.

It has run up so far from the $10.7 trillion at the end of President Bush's term to $14.2 trillion and counting. The debt to GDP ratio is dangerously high now, at 96.3% according to the International Monetary Fund. By the end of 2011 it will amount to 98.6%. The U.S. debt will near $17 trillion and over one hundred percent debt to GDP ratio by the end of President Obama's first term.

How Dangerous is Today's Debt Level in the U.S.?

This debt level is unsustainable for a nation with a AAA credit rating. Economists claim that a Debt to GDP ratio becomes a perilous drain on an economy once this number exceeds ninety percent. The U.S. has been put on credit watch negative as of April 18, 2011 by S&P for good reason. With a budget deficit of nearly $1.5 trillion a year now, and a total debt of $14.3 trillion, S&P may downgrade the AAA rating to AA any day. Does this mean that you can not make money when the debt levels are so dangerously high? Not at all.

How Can You Profit from the Record U.S. Debt Levels of Today?

It is safe to say that the stock market and bond markets are not a good place to hide your investment money if the financial stability of the United States has come into question.

Higher interest rates are in the future for this country. While this will drive down bond yields and crush the stock market, you can be sure that precious metals will soar.

Where can you park your dollars when debt is rising so dangerously fast? Gold and silver are historically the best places to be in times of economic uncertainty, rising inflation, and out of control government spending and money printing. Today is no exception to the rule.

Do you think that the U.S. debt situation has ever called more strongly for precious metals investment than it does today?

The Systematic Destruction of the Western Financial World

When you look at the Western world today, it is easy to lose confidence in what you see. The United States government's credit has been downgraded for the first time in its over two hundred year history. Japan is mired in the aftermath of the Tsunami, nuclear disaster, and attempted recovery.

Europe struggles with its own sovereign government debt problems and possible banking crisis that began in Greece, Portugal, and Ireland and threatens to overtake even Spain and Italy. You have even witnessed Great Britain wrestle with riots, looting, and fires in London and the other major British cities.

In light of all of this chaos that you watch unfold around the various nations of the West, you may feel like this is all too improbable to happen at once.

There is an orchestrated movement that uses these events to push the world towards a new global system of government called the New World Order. In the paragraphs that follow, you will learn why it threatens to overturn the economic and political dominance of the Western World.

What is the New World Order?

The New World Order is a movement to bring all of the the planet under a single cohesive government. This is based on a global agenda to replace the government of sovereign nation states such as the US, France, Russia, Great Britain, China and others with a single totalitarian global governance.

The ideology behind it calls this the highest evolution in the history of the world. To reach this end, the architects behind the New World Order use events in both finance and politics and operate through a number of front organizations to achieve their goals.

What is the History of the New World Order Concept and Movement?

The modern origin of the phrase "New World Order" dates back to American President Woodrow Wilson and World War II era British Prime Minister Winston Churchill. Both men employed the phrase to discuss new historical eras where larger international organizations such as the League of Nations and ultimately the United Nations could prevail.

They believed that as world wars destroyed the planet, people might understand the need for more world governance in order to prevent such destructive conflicts in the future. The hope that these global bodies could supersede petty national interests has only materialized in part, but it was a first step.

Other organizations and protocols were subsequently created in an attempt to move earth toward a new world order of global governance.

NATO, the Breton Woods currency and financial system, NAFTA, the European Union, and the General Agreement on Tariffs and Trade are not mere accidents in this evolution. They were the next steps in the process.

President George H.W. Bush brought back the use of New World Order as a phrase in the 1990's. The G20 and the G7, or Great Twenty nations and Great Seven nations, are incarnations of the movement that attempt to control the world economy in two single sit down organizations that represent the major nations of the world.

The movement really gained traction after the global financial crisis that you saw erupt in 2007. Political leaders British Prime Minister Gordon Brown and revered American statesman Henry Kissinger argued for a new world order as part of the major international reforms that they advocated to reform the world's financial system.

What are the Intentions of the New World Order?

The New World Order will phase out nation states one by one as you see them push towards larger international and supra national treaties and organizations. The movement aims to bring all financial transactions of banks and other institutions under the role of a global super regulator. This has already been approved and signed off on by the West.

You hear discussions to abandon the dollar as the world's reserve currency as one of the chief agendas of the New World Order.

This idea has actually been seriously contemplated at a secretive meeting that France, Russia, China, the Arab oil states, and other nations attended without the U.S. during the Financial Crisis of 2007 to 2009.

Their proposal is to move to a single world currency that no one nation state issues, but that a single world body like the International Monetary Fund manages. They would replace the U.S. dollar with a unit of currency called the SDR's, or special drawing rights of the IMF.

A major obstacle of the New World Order is the super power of the U.S. and its allies. The members of the world wide movement understand that they must remove the U.S. as the world's policeman in order to achieve this.

The New World Order aims to see the nations of the West fade away in favor of a world government. This way the single government will be able to put what it perceives to be the interest of the good above those of individual nationalist interests that cause competition, strife, and inequality.

What Are the Downsides of The New World Order?

There is a real fear among critics of a world government that this New World Order will lead to mass surveillance of people on a level never before seen in history. If you do not believe that this is possible, then consider that democratic Great Britain employs 14 million cameras and adds more daily in order to monitor their sixty million citizens. RFID tags and implantable microchips that the company Digital Angel produces in the United States can track any person who carries them at any time and in any place.

The ability to abuse the power of mass surveillance in order to protect the interests of the greater good is very real already.

The new world order also restricts the rights of individuals to freely practice capitalism. It abhors the idea that a few rogue traders and hedge funds can gang up on a small nation like Greece and attack its bonds in order to make enormous profits. This has happened again and again to countries like Iceland, Portugal, Ireland, and may even spread to Spain and Italy before long.

You may feel that it is your financial right to buy and sell gold, silver, bonds, and stocks freely across the globe. The new world order disagrees if this causes instability, chaos, and panic. This is why you have seen the implementation of naked short selling rules in the United States and Europe. It also explains new regulations in the U.S. called the Frank Dodd Reform Act that prevents people who are residents of the United States from owning Foreign Exchange accounts based in other countries.

Does the New World Order Have any Positive Aspects?

There are some noble goals and intentions of the New World Order. They wish to eradicate disease and poverty on a global scale. The movement plans to stop wars as it eliminates nationalism and the sovereign nation state.

While you may not agree with the disappearance of the United States, Canada, or Britain as political entities, it is hard to argue with the benefits that the architects of the New World Order wish to bring to everyone. The problem will come if you choose to stand in the way of this New World Order.

Have you ever heard the phrase, "The road to hell is paved with good intentions?"

What Happens When The Government Debt Bubble Pops?

In the next ten years, you are going to look back and realize that the Great Recession actually marked the beginning of the end of the present financial system and dollar hegemony that has existed in the world since the Second World War.

This will be brought about by the sudden loss of confidence in the U.S. led world economy. When the government debt bubble finally pops, the stage will be fully set for the dollar to drop rapidly and drastically. You may be wondering how the dollar came to be in a bubble in the first place.

The bubble in the dollar came about as a result of President Nixon ending the U.S. dollar alignment to the gold standard back in 1971. Until that point, the dollar contained an intrinsic value that was equivalent to a certain amount of gold kept in government vaults. This provided the dollar with great stability year in and year out.

The Loss of Intrinsic Value

When the United States abandoned the gold standard, the dollar instantly lost all of its intrinsic value and entered a multiple decade bear market from which it has never recovered nor escaped.

The end result of this has been a consistent and long term erosion of the dollar's value, interspersed by periodic bear market rallies. As these bear market rallies took place, it was easy for you and most Americans to forget that a bear market in the dollar continued to rage.

You might even have become convinced that the Dollar is a safe haven in the meanwhile. This is an all too common false perception, since the rallies in the bear market of the dollar calmed down investors to the point that they were blindsided every time as the bear market in the greenback resumed.

Finally, this bear market in the dollar will reach its epic low as the majority of Americans and even foreign investors have become the victims of intense losses on all assets that are denominated in dollars. This means that U.S. stocks, bonds, real estate, Treasuries, and CD's will all suffer the same fate at that time, since they are all investments whose values are related in terms of dollars.

The End of This Financial System Is Near

Along with the end of the dollar as a reserve currency will come the end of the present financial system. This event will be far reaching in its impacts and effects. As oil, gold, silver, and other commodities are no longer priced in dollars at that point, the affordability of these essential commodities will skyrocket for all Americans.

Banks and Central Banks will dump their dollar reserves for some other currency that will have to arise to replace the dollar. Right now, the only contenders for this position of alternative reserve currency are either the Euro or gold and silver.

Naturally, the end of the dollar as the world's reserve currency will entail a great amount of pain and loss of wealth for the typical American. Imports, including energy, will become horrifically expensive as the dollar resets to a far lower value. Foreign travel will likely once more become a luxury of the wealthy, as it was in times past. The dislocation in the U.S. economy will cause many industries to contract substantially, leading to an unemployment rate that will likely make today's near ten percent unemployment look respectable.

The Impact on Foreign Countries

Foreign countries will also be dramatically impacted by the end of the present financial system and dollar. Those whose economies are heavily based on exports, particularly to the U.S., will also be in a great deal of trouble. This includes Germany and Japan principally. Those with large holdings of U.S. Dollars and dollar denominated debt will also suffer severe setbacks. This includes China and most of the oil rich Arab sultanates of the Middle East. Their enormous and impressive stock piles of U.S. treasuries at that point will be kindling for fire wood.

It is obvious that this change to a new financial system and world reserve currency will be difficult. Even though the American people will bear the brunt of the adjustment, foreigners will similarly suffer in the upheaval. This is particularly the case for those countries that are tied most closely to the U.S. economy, trade, and economic system.

Please Mister, Can You Spare a Hundred Bucks?

All of these monumental changes that are already in motion in the world economy and financial system will actually transpire over the next five years. In that time span, you will see the U.S. government debt scheme fail and the U.S. dollar purchasing power go to pieces. When this happens, you can count on the U.S. government attempting to print its way out of the crisis initially. It will come down to a choice of this or not paying the bills for domestic spending like Medicare and Social Security.

Over the last few years, the government has already demonstrated its ability and willingness to majorly increase the money supply in an attempt to restore the falling economy and to pay for stimulus. They have done this to the tune of a three hundred percent increase to the total U.S. Dollar base money supply around the world.

Imagine how much farther they will be willing to go with the electronic printing press when things get really bad, for example when the proverbial U.S. treasury bill unlimited spending credit card is rejected by the foreign investors.

If the U.S. no longer has anyone to buy its debt and loan it money, then it will be left with the other alternative of simply printing more money to cover the increasing shortfalls. While the government can and does simply print extra money to pay the bills and for spending, there is a consequence for engaging in these actions, particularly when they start increasing the number of available dollars exponentially.

Inflation Is Always A Currency Driven Event

Inflation is always the product of too many paper bills chasing too few goods and services; this is why it is called a currency driven event. You have not yet seen the effects and results of these actions from the last round of money printing that went on in the last few years.

When the government attempts to create really enormous quantities of lower valued dollars to pay for things, then you will see hyperinflation of the currency. Hyperinflation is typically in the hundreds of percent per year, though it can reach hundreds and even thousands of percent per month as governments resort increasingly to printing more and more money in a vain attempt to solve their problems. You may say that hyperinflation could never happen in the United States, but the truth is that it already has on three separate occasions.

During the Revolutionary War, the new American government saw its continental dollars succumb to the ravages of hyperinflation as they printed too many of them to pay for the war. In the Civil War, hyperinflation also reared its ugly head, particularly in the Confederacy of the South. President Franklin Roosevelt also invited hyperinflation in 1933 when he devalued the dollar by fifty percent against gold. In some instances of hyperinflation in places like post World War I Germany, paper money has become so worthless that a wheelbarrow of it is necessary to purchase a single loaf of bread.

Hyperinflation causes many terrible effects for a nation and its people. Not the least of them is the encouragement to spend all money as soon as it is earned and received, since it will be worth less the next day.

Savers Are Ruined by Hyperinflation

Savers are ruined by hyperinflation, particularly those who are stuck on fixed incomes, such as retirees. Economic activity also suffers badly for lack of price and wage stability within the economy and an uncertain future outlook. Jobs are lost as part of the effects, and many important goods become unaffordable for many people.

Hyperinflation does not go on forever. When the government that is responsible for it begins raising interest rates and stops printing money, it settles down and an economy gradually returns to normal. Unfortunately, many people are ruined by such hyperinflation before it is brought back under control.

The good news is that one of the few investments that does not suffer from hyperinflation actually thrives in it. This is silver and gold. Precious metals are your ultimate protection against the coming instability and hyperinflation of the next few years. Once it starts, their present values will appear astonishingly cheap.

Politics

<u>HISTORY</u>

"Events That Shaped Our Present"

History

An Inside Look Into The Masters of The Financial Sandbox

Undoubtedly you have experienced your share of curiosity and frustration over the last few years as you witnessed the world financial system nearly collapse and the economy melt down. What you may not have understood is how these events actually took place.

The book "Extreme Money: Masters of the Universe and the Cult of Risk," by Satyajit Das, attempts to explain what transpired and who is responsible for the destruction of your 401k, your retirement dreams, and possibly your job.

In the paragraphs below, you will understand why this book is a must read, not only so that you can point fingers and take names, but so that you can learn why the economic events that continue to unfold actually do so.

About the Author Satyajit Das

Satyajit Das the author is an internationally renowned finance expert who claims more than thirty years of business and finance experience. Mr. Das has worked on behalf of the buyers in finance in the capacity as TNT Group Treasurer.

He has also provided services to the sellers in finance when he worked for Merrill Lynch and Citicorp Investment Bank. Besides this, he has served as a consultant to investors, banks, central banks, and corporations across the globe.

Satyajit Das is one of those rare individuals who foretold a number of the events that surrounded the worldwide financial meltdown. He did this in his 2006 book "Traders, Guns, and Money: Knowns and Unknowns in the Dazzling World of Derivatives." Besides this, he gave a speech the same year entitled "The Coming Credit Crash," where he attempted to warn investors of the writing that was already on the wall.

Das has numerous impressive credits to his name. He appeared as a featured expert in the 2010 Oscar winning, Charles Ferguson documentary, "Inside Job." He has also been in the BBC Television's 2009 documentary, "Tricks with Risk." He has written a number of well thought of works on risk management and derivatives, the highly leveraged and toxic financial instruments that blew up the world financial system.

Among these are the 2005 editions of Swaps/Financial Derivatives Library, an exhaustive encyclopedia-like reference work for derivatives traders; and Credit Derivatives, CDO's, & Structured Credit Products. On top of this, Satyajit Das has written extensively about financial topics in newspapers and professional publications.

You can see Satyajit Das on television and hear him on radio in countries like the United States, Great Britain, Canada, Australia, New Zealand, South Africa, and India. He writes opinion pieces for such gold standard publications as the Financial Times of London.

You might have read his posts on well known financial websites and blogs such as www.roubini.com, www.nakedcapitalism.com, www.minyanville.com, www.prudentbear.com, www.eurointelligence.com, and www.wilmott.com. There is no doubt that when the author Satyajit Das speaks, he has earned your attention and careful consideration.

What is the Premise of "Extreme Money?"

"Extreme Money" begins with an interesting premise. Mankind created both money and finance. For good or ill, these inventions have changed us in their turn. You and all of humanity misunderstood the purpose of money. It should have only been the oil that lubricated the machine of humanity and civilization's well being. Instead, money has become an end goal all by itself, rather than simply the means to enjoy your life.

Worse than this common misunderstanding of money is the somewhat complicated concept of finance. Author Das defines finance as the monetary shadow of tangible, real things. Sadly, this finance world has become the master of all human existence around the globe. "Extreme Money" sets out to explain the story of the way that this happened. This is not just a history lesson; it is the tale of the entire modern world in which you live and work.

Mr. Das knows this financial world better than most, as he has spent over thirty-three years of his own life in the center of current day global finance. From this insider's point of view, he shares the story with you. He unveils the incredible, amazing, and perilous games that the financial masters of the universe play with money.

These exciting and high stakes diversions have blown up enormous and destructive bubbles of Ponzi scheme prosperity, false growth pictures, enormous wealth, and lavish lifestyles on the back of regular, ordinary working people's livelihoods, jobs, futures, and material possessions. You, the common man and woman, are the biggest losers in this high stakes game that you have little control over or even any knowledge about.

What Can You Learn from "Extreme Money?"

Satyajit Das has much to teach you about in this insightful work. He explains the way that every element, from world wide climate change to the mortgage on your house, is now a financial transaction. In the process, enormous fortunes are created by people who do not built up anything of real, tangible, or lasting value.

He instructs you about extreme money and the reasons that it is unreal. He shows you that what he calls "voodoo banking" makes incredible profits that are only on paper for banks even to this day. He reveals the secrets of hedge funds, derivatives, the packaging up of loans and mortgages, and the inner working of debt instruments and little known yet common banking practices.

Perhaps most upsetting to you will be the realization that these incredibly young "Masters of the Financial Universe" control practically the entire world, whether you like it or not.

What is the Final Verdict of Extreme Money?

Author Das' work "Extreme Money" shines a telling light into the dark recesses of financial alchemy, where young but powerful individuals work in the shadows to make enormous fortunes at the expense of the rest of you.

It lays bare the investment bankers' schemes and machinations which culminated in the worldwide financial crisis and Great Recession of 2007 to date. As such, it is an illuminating text that has much to teach you about the world of high finance.

This does not mean that it is an easy read by any means. While it does go straight to the heart of these important topics about finance and power, it is involved and sometimes complex. You will be challenged and made to think, if you take the time to read about the rise and ongoing rule of financial power brokers and their shadowy but lavish financial underworld.

Legendary economist and New York University Economics Professor Nouriel Roubini, who also predicted the financial crisis years ago, says that author Satyajit Das gives you a real inside appreciation for the financial sandbox that the financial masters of the universe played and worked in during the past thirty years.

He shows you the terrible results of their wealth-making fun and games. The writer brings an up close and personal experience to the financial world and demonstrates to you the way that it really works. When you read the book for yourself, you will finally understand how this world that you share with billions of other individuals came to be in today's financial mess.

"Extreme Money" does not answer the question of where we go from here. It also does not leave you with a sense of optimism about the near term economic future of the world. The solutions may not be so easy.

Do you have any idea how we can get out of this ongoing financial tragedy?

The Consequences After 40 Years Without Gold Standard

You may not remember that forty years ago the United States left the gold standard in favor of a fiat currency whose value is based on simply the faith in and credit of the U.S. government.

This defiant move that shook the world monetary and financial systems resulted from a little known secret that you are probably unaware of, as are most other people.

In the paragraphs that follow, you will come to understand not only the dark secret that caused the U.S. to abandon the gold standard, but also the terrible consequences that have impacted the economy in the forty years that followed.

Why Did the U.S. Leave the Gold Standard?

The U.S. banking system hides a little known, even dirty, secret that forced the United States to abandon the gold standard back in 1971. The dollar was backed up by gold ounces valued at $35 in paper money until 1971.

This helped to keep the value of the dollar incredibly stable, as gold and silver are the only consistent real forms of money that have always held their value over the long term, throughout all history. The gold standard should have limited the number of paper dollars that existed to the amount of gold reserves in U.S. government vaults.

The secret is that banks and the Federal Reserve have the power to create more money out of thin air. This is called the fractional reserve banking system.

In 1971, banks and the Fed had conspired together to create many more dollars than the U.S. government could comfortably back up with the gold that they physically owned. That year, France and Great Britain called Uncle Sam's bluff and demanded that the U.S. exchange its paper dollars for gold at the set rate of $35 per ounce.

The U.S. under President Nixon refused to relinquish all of its valuable gold for the oversupplied U.S. dollars that foreign governments held. So Richard Nixon did the only thing that he could do in this particular situation and abandoned the gold standard in order to protect and maintain the country's true wealth, its still vast gold reserves.

What Have the Consequences Been Forty Years Later?

Thanks to President Nixon's move, the United States can still claim to have the world's largest gold reserves at more than eight thousand metric tons. Unfortunately for the national economy, there were terrible consequences that resulted from turning your money into worthless green paper.

Since that fateful day forty years ago when your dollars ceased to be exchangeable for gold and became only empty promises from an increasingly debt strapped government, you have seen a terrible and devastating decline in the standard of living for the vast majority of Americans. Read on to see how this single event created historic inflation, minimum wages and jobs that have actually declined against the higher cost of living, runaway housing and gasoline prices, lower personal savings rates, and a decline in the real purchasing power of your dollar in general.

Inflation Since 1971

The best way to measure the change in inflation is to look at a good inflation calculator. The U.S. inflation calculator tells you that an item that you purchased in 1971 for $100 would cost you $557.83 in 2011.

That is a rate of inflation of 457.8% in forty years.

That may not sound like much, but when you average it out over forty years, it gives you an average annual inflation rate of over eleven percent per year. These numbers are based on the government's official rates of inflation formulas too, and are not at all inflated to compensate for the tricks that the government has routinely employed to disguise real inflation rates in the U.S.

Minimum Wages Since 1971

Consider the minimum wage that acts as the basic standard of living floor for millions of Americans who count themselves lucky to have any job at all in the economy of today. In 1971, the minimum wage stood at $1.60 per hour. In 2011, it has risen to $7.25 per hour. That sounds like an impressive rise over forty years, as it has literally risen by 353% over the last forty years. Inflation has risen almost thirty percent more than the minimum wages.

In very real and painful terms, people who lived on minimum wages in 1971 have watched their present day minimum wage decline so steeply that they can not live on them anymore, even if they have two minimum wage earners in a family. Perhaps this helps to explain why one in five Americans requires food stamps from the government today in order to have enough food.

Job Salaries Since 1971

You might argue that the average income of Americans has risen far more dramatically than minimum wages over the last forty years since the country left the gold standard. The truth reveals a different picture. In 1971, the average annual income for American workers stood at $10,600. Today, this job's salary pays $43,460 on average for men and $35,102 for women.

This means that the average salary for males has increased by only 310%, a number that is actually less than the change in the minimum wage since 1971. For women, the salaries have risen by around 230% in forty years. These numbers are abysmal when compared to the rise in inflation that is up over 457% in the same time frame.

Housing Costs Since 1971

The average cost of a new house in 1971 stood at $25,250. In August of 2011, it hovers around $212,400. Average home values have risen a dramatic 741% in forty years. This is fantastic if you own the same home that you purchased in 1971 or earlier. For people who are just in the market to buy one now, your salaries have risen an average of only 270% since 1971. This means that you will pay nearly three times as much for a house that you did in constant 1971 earnings and dollars.

Gasoline Prices Since 1971

Do you remember when gas cost only forty cents per gallon back in 1971? Forty years later, it averages at $3.62 per gallon. This is an increase of 805% in the price that you pay at the pump over forty years. Your average salary increase of 270% in the same time is not leaving you much money to fill your gas tank.

Personal Savings Rate Since 1971

The personal savings rate is a formula that you figure up when you subtract your expense from your income. The money that you have left and do not spend at the end of the month is counted as personal savings. In 1971, with the dollar solidly backed by gold still, you saved an average of 10% after expenses. In 2011, this amount sits at 5.2% for the average person. Thanks to the declining real value of your earnings, you are not able to save as much as you once did.

Purchasing Power of the Dollar Since 1971

The most obvious proof that when the U.S. departed from the gold standard, it destroyed the dollar and the economy are evident when you look at the price of gold since 1971. Gold has posted highs and lows over the decades, but it has always remained far higher than the 1971 price of gold at $35 when the U.S. still honored the gold standard.

In August 2011, gold is at more than $1,800 per ounce. To put this in terms that will make your blood run cold, your U.S. dollars have *declined by over 98% against the yellow metal* in those forty years since we turned our back on the most precious of metals.

In light of these many sad revelations about the economy since we left the gold standard in 1971, what would you rather own five years from today, $50,000 worth of paper bills backed by the full credit of the U.S. government, or $50,000 worth of gold that are valued in today's dollar?

<u>MONEY</u>

"Understanding the Medium of Exchange"

Money

5 Effective Debt Relief Solutions You May Want to Consider

by James Alexander

A lot of people find themselves in so much debt that they will never be able to escape, or so they believe. Most of these people begin accruing debt through credit cards. These, easy to use, cards allow people to spend a lot of money, with a minimal amount of effort.

People do not feel the same effect when they swipe a card, as they do when spending cash. The simple reason for this is because they do not see their checking account take an instant hit. The problem is that they get used to spending all of this money when they are in a solid economic position.

However, when the economy plummets, people may find themselves unemployed and unable to pay their credit card bill. The worst problem is that they will likely still use their card, as they have to buy food and pay bills, despite being out of a job.

What a Debt Relief Specialist Does

A debt relief specialist will consult with clients about their debt scenario. While people may believe that credit card debt for one person is the same for another, it is actually not the case.

There are people, who realize that they are in major problems after a few months, while others wait several years to ask for assistance.

It would, obviously, be ideal to receive assistance as early as possible, as this will prevent the debt from accruing to a high amount. A debt relief specialist will have years of experience in analyzing client's finances, so they will be able to help in several ways. The first thing they will do is to analyze the client's personal finances. They will want to know which lenders are owed money, as well as the income and expenses of their client.

It is important for the specialist to have honest documents regarding these things, as this will allow them to help the customer. They are essentially going to try and help the customer get out of debt, while making it as affordable as possible. It will be more difficult for them to construct a settlement if they do not understand the client's actual financial situation.

Negotiating a Settlement

Most debt relief specialists will be able to negotiate with credit card companies. However, it is important that the specialist knows the client's situation, as lenders are less willing to negotiate if they view the negotiation as a game. The way this scenario typically works is that the specialist and the lender will negotiate a payment plan that will work for both parties.

The lender is going to want to collect as much money as possible, since it is their money that is not being returned. However, the specialist will be able to explain the client's situation to the lenders, which will allow them to settle for a lesser amount.

People will find that most lenders are not willing to construct a settlement with an individual, so this is why it is important to have a specialist's assistance. People will usually have 36 months to pay their debt off, and they will be considered in good-standing again. This is the preferred method, as it typically does not harm one's credit score.

Credit Counseling

Credit counseling is another, popular, method used by many debt relief specialists. This is similar to a debt settlement; however, it typically applies to those, who are making their payment. Most of these people are simply disturbed by the high interest rates.

A lot of people find that it is extremely difficult to get a creditor to lower interest rates, as this is where they make the majority of their money. In fact, credit card companies do not like customers, who pay their bills on time. A debt relief specialist may be able to help clients negotiate a lower interest rate.

Miscellaneous

There are several other options for getting out of debt, which range from using retirement accounts to consolidating payments. Many people like these plans, as it will allow them to borrow against their possessions. However, this is sort of a last resort thing, as people do not want to have anything repossessed.

Consider Bankruptcy

Bankruptcy should be a last resort for people who are in a ton of debt. There are two types of bankruptcy, which are commonly referred to as Chapter 7 and Chapter 13.

Chapter 7 allows people to get completely out of debt. Chapter 13 allows people to consolidate their payments and eventually work their way out of debt. Chapter 13 is the better option of the two, as people will typically not have anything repossessed.

People should always consult with a specialist before making any of these financial moves. This will allow them to have an expert review their scenario, which will likely yield a better result. By following the proper program, people can get back to living a normal, debt free life in a few years.

Author Bio:

James Alexander is an author of finance, money management and debt relief solutions related articles. He's an author for more than 1 year and until now he's working on good articles with reliable tips and advices that will help those people who are in debt.
www.debtfreedestiny.com

What You Need To Know About The Euro Currency Crisis

When you turn on the news or pick up a newspaper these days, you invariably see a headline about the Euro currency crisis. This crisis only seems to get worse with every week and news update. Just a few days ago, Jacques Delors, the former President of the European Commission, declared that the Eurozone itself stands on the edge of the abyss.

You may wonder if there is a way that you can profit from this crisis of confidence in the Euro single currency. Below, you will learn what countries use the Euro, what the crisis is all about, whether the crisis will lead to the breakup of the Euro zone itself, and how you can use Exchange Traded Funds to take advantage of the situation and profit.

What Countries Use the Euro?

The Euro is the single European Union currency that is now utilized by seventeen different sovereign nations on the continent. While there are twenty-seven nations in the European Union itself, ten of them either do not use the Euro yet, such as most of the Eastern European EU countries, or are not required to adopt the Euro at all, as in the case of Sweden, Denmark, and the United Kingdom.

The seventeen countries that presently have the Euro as their national currencies include:

- Germany
- France
- Italy
- Spain
- The Netherlands
- Belgium
- Luxembourg
- Austria
- Cyprus
- Finland
- Estonia
- Greece
- Ireland
- Malta
- Portugal
- Slovenia
- Slovakia

What Is Happening With the Euro and the Euro Zone?

The Euro has been one of the stronger currencies against the dollar in the last ten years. In the years since the financial crisis erupted, a cloud has appeared over the currency. Some of the nations in the Euro zone block have evolved into a drag on the common currency. Investors and analysts have affectionately nicknamed these slower growth, lower productivity, Southern European countries the PIIGS, or Portugal, Ireland, Italy, Greece, and Spain.

Several of these PIIGS nations have recently experienced terrible investor loss of confidence in their economies that continue to struggle in the aftermath of the Great Recession that began in 2007 and continues to grind away four years later. You may heard something about the near financial collapse of Greece that had to be bailed out to the tune of hundreds of billions of dollars in order to avoid default on all of its sovereign debt and the debt of its various banks.

You may not be aware that the same series of events has overtaken Ireland and Portugal in the last year as well. Both of these sovereign nations also had to be bailed out with sums that amounted to well over one hundred billion dollars as well. Now the rumor is that both trillion dollar economy Spain and even mighty Italy, a member of the G7 group of seven richest nations on earth, may also need major financial life lines thrown to them as the European sovereign and banking debt crisis continues to spread its contagion.

All of these crisis of confidence events that have overrun the majority of the PIIGS and threaten to overturn even Spain and Italy exact a heavy toll on confidence on the Euro. The crisis has become so bad that Germany's most respected major newspaper Der Spiegel recently claimed that the Euro simply can not survive in the present day form. The newspaper added that some of the nations in the Euro will be forced to leave if the European Union is to survive and thrive.

Will Some Countries Really Leave the Euro Behind?

It is not easy to abandon the currency that all your consumers, businesses, government agencies, and banks use on a daily basis.

There is a very real fear that it could spark a run on the banks of the nations who choose to do so. In such a case, investors in those respective countries that left it would probably demand Euros, Dollars, Pounds, and Swiss Francs for their bank deposits instead of potentially revived Greek Drachmas, Italian Liras, or Irish Pounds.

Still, there is more talk that Germany and France, the two economic growth engines and powerhouses of the Euro currency zone, will either decide to leave the other nations of the Euro behind as they form a more tightly knit fiscal and monetary union themselves, or they will find a way to change the Euro zone rules so that the weaker sister nations of the PIIGS have no choice but to leave. The third alternative that some analysts have thrown down is that Germany itself might leave the Euro and return to the German Mark that became the basis for the Euro in the first place.

How Many More Bailouts Can the Euro Take?

The Eurozone and the European Central Bank have worked with the International Monetary Fund to set up the European Stability Mechanism, or ESM in 2011. This much larger fund has more than five hundred billion dollars worth of new money to throw at the problem. In theory, this means that the Euro zone might be able to bail out Spain, but probably not Italy, and certainly not Italy and Spain combined.

The real answer to the question of how many more bailouts that the Euro can withstand comes down to the German people. Germany represents the biggest and highest growth rate economy in the Euro Zone. As such, it backs over one fourth of the costs for these bailouts of other weaker Euro Zone countries.

Angela Merkel, the Premier of Germany, has continued to stand up for the poorer and smaller economies of the Euro Zone so far. For better or worse though, her popularity continues to erode, and her government loses local by election after election as each of these turns into a referendum on the Euro bailout policies.

How low can the Euro go?

You may feel like you ought to be able to play this trade on the Euro with your investments. If you feel that the Euro will decline as the crisis plays out, then you should know the lows that the Euro might reach. From its early September 2011 range of $1.38 to $1.46, it could drop to the several year low set back during the financial crisis. At this time, the Euro fell to just below $1.19 against the dollar.

In theory, it could drop back to its all time low of below 1:1 with the dollar. This is highly unlikely, though.

There is also the strong possibility that Germany and France will go the Euro alone without the weaker nations of the south. In this case, the Euro could easily rise to from $1.70 to $2.00. You should consider the very real possibility that the crisis will only last until either a closer monetary union led by Germany is hammered out, or Germany kicks out the weaker nations. Anyone who studies the history of the "European Project" can tell you that the elite class of rulers in Europe simply will not let the European Union and common Euro currency fail.

What are Good Exchange Traded Funds to Profit from the Euro Crisis?

Whichever way you decide to play the Euro currency crisis, you can easily do it if you purchase one of several Euro Exchange Traded Funds. These trade exactly like stocks on major stock exchanges. They allow you to buy, sell, and use limit and stop orders to protect any profits and limit your losses. Two of the good ones are the FXE, or Currency Shares Euro Trust, and the ERO, or iPath EUR/USD Exchange Rate ETF's.

The biggest personal investment question that you have to ask yourself with regards to the Euro Zone crisis of confidence is this - will you bet on the Euro or against it?

Numis Network - Silver Coin of the Month Club Review

If you have ever considered the possibility that you might purchase some silver coins to have in your portfolio of investments, then you may have thought about the fun that you could have if you acquired silver collectible coins.

The decision to collect silver coins that are numismatic, or somewhat rare and collectible, instead of to acquire bullion coins, or coins that have no value beyond their silver content, is one that you should consider carefully.

One thing that you have to keep in mind is that there is a significant extra cost that you will incur if you choose to go the collectible silver coin route. A company that offers you an innovative approach to the collectible coin market is Numis Network. You will read all about their products, services, and network in the paragraphs below.

What is the Silver Coin of the Month Club?

Numis Network calls their featured product and service the Silver Coin of the Month Club. When you decide to join this program, you get a collectible type of silver coin in the mail every month.

These are known as either numismatic or semi-numismatic coins, as they are mostly bullion coins that various governments of the world mint in present times and then sell in near perfect quality to companies like Numis Network.

The Numis people then take these coins and have them professionally graded and certified. The companies that grade these coins seal them up in airtight plastic containers so that your museum quality condition coin stays that way for all time, or at least for as long as you do not let the hard plastic container get damaged or punctured.

You will see that there are some advantages to this service. You can acquire silver coins each and every month at a price that they set based on the spot market price of silver the month prior to when they send you the coin. This means that an October coin's price will be set based on the price of silver at the end of September.

You do not have to have knowledge of the coin industry in order to collect semi-numismatic coins this way. The idea is that you will acquire silver coins that should appreciate in value over time, especially as silver prices continue to rise in the years that come.

The clear downside to this program is that Numis Network is able to charge enormous markup prices on their silver coins simply because they are semi-numismatic, or occasionally numismatic, in nature. A real example from their site is that when the silver spot price trades between $40 and $49.99 in October, then you can expect to pay $129.95 for the silver coin that comes conveniently to your mailbox in November.

Money

You may be someone who really enjoys the opportunity to collect these beautiful silver coins. There is satisfaction in the hobby. Just remember that you will pay an $80 premium over the spot value of silver in order to do this. There are much more economical ways to acquire silver coins for investment purposes.

What is the Fast Track Collector's Kit?

Another product that Numis Network sincerely recommends to you is their Fast Track Collector's Kit. Should you decide to purchase this kit, you will receive a beautiful attache case that helps you to carry, protect, and show off your silver coin of the month club collection.

The kit comes with a present day silver collectible coin from somewhere around the world in MS70, or certified one hundred percent perfect, condition. You also get a "Coins are Cool" series of DVD's that are a featured part of their educational library. Besides this, your kit comes with Numis Network's "Forever Crystal" that allows you to etch a memory or special words in to crystal.

This is a beautiful set to own. If your goal is to build up a silver coin collection that you wish to show off to the world, then you may choose to go with this product. Just remember that you will pay a hefty premium over the spot price of silver for this collection. That makes far more sense for a silver coin collector than for a silver investor.

What Graded Gold and Silver Coins Does Numis Network Offer?

Numis Coins also offers you an extensive array of both silver and gold coins that both the U.S. Mint and other well known nations of the world produce.

When you consider these coins, you will be able to choose from American Gold and Silver Eagles minted in different U.S. mints around the country.

You will also have choices of first strike and limited edition coins that other government mints produce. You will find coins in their catalog that Austria, Great Britain, Canada, China, Australia, Mexico and others produce. They will be certified and graded by either PCGS, NGC, or ANACS, the three professional coin graders that are universally recognized and accepted.

What is the Numis Gift Set?

The Numis Gift Set is a coin set that includes your picture, words, and thoughts that you choose to have etched on to their Forever Crystal product. It comes in a beautiful wooden gift box. You can choose whichever coins to go with the set that you wish.

What is the Numis Network Opportunity About?

Numis Network also offers you the opportunity to become an affiliate and to help them sell the Silver Coin of the Month Club. They provide you with retail commissions, a one hundred dollar fast track bonus, a preferred customer sales bonus, and a Silver Eagle bonus pool, as well as various other bonuses and rewards from time to time.

In order to become an Independent Collector Representative, you would be expected to purchase the Fast Track Collectors Kit so that you are able to demonstrate the coin products to your potential clients and other representatives who will join your personal marketing network.

If you are able to convince your friends, neighbors, and associates to collect coins via the Silver Coin of the Month Club, then you can anticipate potentially significant current income as well as possibly substantial residual income in the future. Like with any multi level marketing scheme, this requires a great deal of persistence, patience, and sales skills with other people.

What is the Five Year Buyback Guarantee and How Does it Work?

Numis Network does offer one incredible guarantee that should give you some peace of mind if you decide to purchase their significantly marked up semi-numismatic or numismatic silver and gold coins. This is called the Five Year Buy Back Guarantee. They declare this to be a totally unique and the most superior buy back offer in the coin industry.

If at the end of the five years from your purchase date, you decide that you do not like the coins, or more likely that you paid too much for them, then you have an additional one hundred and twenty days from the five year anniversary date of your purchase to return these coins to the Numis Network dealer.

They will give you a full refund of your purchase price. This guarantee only applies to any coins that you purchase in the Silver Coin of the Month Club. Naturally, the coins and their hard plastic cases that they come encased in must be in perfect and undamaged condition in order for Numis to accept them back.

What is the Refund Policy of Numis Network?

Numis also offers a full thirty day money back guarantee on any numismatic coins that you buy. If you change your mind, they will allow you to return all undamaged and in original condition coins to them. This is a reasonable return policy for the industry.

Now that you know all about Numis Network and their products and services, you have to decide for yourself how much over the actual spot price of silver you are willing to pay in order to enjoy collectible semi-numismatic and numismatic coins.

Numis Network:

www.numisnetwork.com

Can You Use Debt To Improve Your Financial Situation?

You would not be alone any more if you experience money problems. Personal debt levels have become one of the great embarrassments of the United States' and other Western capitalist economies over the last forty years.

The rise of credit cards and personal loans that were all too easy to obtain over the last few decades has aggravated the financial and economic crisis to a very dangerous point. The good news is that there is hope for you to escape from your own money problems.

In the paragraphs below, you will see why your goal should not be to get out of debt, but instead should be to use debt in the correct way to improve your overall personal financial situation.

Your Financial Situation Does Not Improve When You Obsess About Your Debt

You may think that the best way to get your personal financial house in order is to concentrate on your debt. There are several problems with this line of thought. When you obsess over your debt, it does not lead you on to phenomenal success with money. You focus on the problem instead of the solution.

If you hone in on the obstacle and not the answer, then you set yourself up for psychological failure. The truth is that when you think about debt all of the time, you actually spawn more of the debt that you hate and struggle to eliminate.

The same is true when you try to lose weight and diet. As with debt obsession, everyone seems to be interested in a way to lose weight these days. You focus on how many calories that you take in, how many carbohydrates that Beach Diet, or some other latest diet fad. The point is that you can only lose weight if the goal is not to lose weight, but to have a healthy body that is both lean and flexible. In other words, natural and comprehensive exercise is the solution to your weight problems, not a diet or obsession over the food that you eat each meal.

How Will a Wealthy You Look Like?

To continue with the diet and fitness analogy, you should think about not only how a healthy you will look in the future, but how a wealthy you will appear one day. In order to do this, you need to set medium as well as long term goals for your financial future. You can start when you sit down and list out where you want to be with your finances a year from now.

But do not stop there. Think about what your financial profile ought to be in two years and five years. Then once you have successfully mapped these time frames out, think long term. Where will you be in ten years, twenty years, and even fifty years from now with your finances? This is the first step to prepare yourself for a wealthier you down the road.

What Are the Differences Between Bad and Good Debts?

Now once you focus on your financial health and you motivate yourself to get rid of your debt, you have to understand and internalize the second, more critical step. You must now make efforts to get out of bad debt, not all debt.

Believe it or not, some debt is actually good. Debts that are bad are the ones that cost you money every month in interest and negative cash flow, or that cause money to leave your accounts. Credit card bills, car payments, and sometimes even mortgage payments are prime examples of these things that can be negative for your financial health.

On the other hand, debts that allow you to purchase and control assets which produce income and create positive cash flow are quite positive for your financial health. As an example, if you buy an income property to rent out, you gain income tax break advantages, have cash flow that comes in every month, and hopefully also make some profit.

With this rental property income, you might save up enough money to use good debt to purchase a second, third, and even fourth property to rent out and bring in still more money. Finally, you can live off of the rental income that your good debts helped you to generate over time. Good debts will allow you to acquire more wealth. You must not be afraid of the right kind of debt.

Why Is All Money Debt Today?

Another reason not to fear good debts is that all money is debt since 1971 anyway. Until 1971, all money in the Western World existed as notes that were convertible into gold and/or silver on demand.

Then President Richard Nixon abandoned the gold standard and instantly destroyed the real value of the currency. He did this because he had no choice. The U.S. fractional reserve banking system had been quietly expanding the money supply at a much faster pace than the country's gold reserves had grown.

Finally, Britain and France caught on to this Ponzi scheme that the U.S. government had been operating for a few years and demanded that the American government honor the paper dollars for gold exchange at the then current fixed price of gold at $35 per ounce.

The government had two choices. It could allow its bluff with the money supply to be called and see the world's largest gold reserves be depleted in a matter of months and years. Otherwise, they could choose as President Nixon did and change the rules of the game. Nixon declared the gold standard unilaterally ended by the United States. In one swift move, he both saved the nation's invaluable gold supply and totally debased the value of all U.S. money from that point forward.

Practically every other country of the world followed suit in a matter of months, and soon all money on earth had become mere paper backed by empty promises. Switzerland remained the notable lone exception as their constitution requires them to keep a 1:4 ratio of gold to Swiss Francs in their vaults. They value their gold reserves at around $250 per ounce, which means that with real gold prices in the $1,500-$1,900 range, they have covered their paper Swiss Francs with a 150% and higher real gold value to Swiss Francs ratio.

This otherwise unanimous debasement changed all money into debts issued by the full faith and credit of the U.S. and other world governments.

Since paper currencies aside from the Swiss Franc are no longer backed by anything, they are also not worth anything tangible. Governments no longer constrained by a monetary limit based on gold and silver reserves can print as many paper and electronic bills as they want, and they practice this very well.

No longer backed up by gold and silver reserves, paper bills today are merely empty promises of increasingly bankrupt governments. Because of this tragic series of events that Nixon put into motion forty years ago, all money since 1971 is nothing but debt.

Do not become confused by the misleading concept that all debt is bad. If all debt is bad nowadays, then so is all money. Would you rather learn to use good debt wisely and solve your money problems or instead continue to treat all debt as bad and drown in the misery of your negative debt?

Money

<u>**TOOLS**</u>

"Instruments for Building a Wealth Foundation"

Five of The Best Places to Purchase Gold and Silver

It is hard for you to miss the news that gold hit yet another all time high of over $1,787 per ounce on August 10.

As gold and silver continue their bull market run that has extended for more than ten years now, you may think that it is time for you to finally buy into the precious metals.

It is important that you find a reputable and helpful gold and silver dealer when you make this decision so that the experience is as easy and convenient as possible. In the following paragraphs, you will read about five of the best places to purchase gold and silver, what sets them apart from the competition, and what their various strengths and weaknesses are.

Monex

Monex bills itself as the leading outfit for gold and silver in America. They have established a trustworthy reputation in the bullion and coin business for over forty years. They are also among the largest gold and silver dealers with over thirty billion dollars in precious metals traded with clients over the decades. The Carabini family that started the firm still runs it. There are now three generations of them who work in the business.

The Monex outfit operates among the easiest to use and best websites for your gold and silver purchases. On their site, you will find helpful videos on the precious metals that you might be interested to purchase. They pride themselves on the information that they give you on all of the products that you might consider. The selection of metals offered by Monex is also strong. Each item's price is clearly listed. Website design is certainly their top forte at Monex.

There are a few downsides to Monex. They have a lesser bullion inventory than some of the other major precious metals outfits. The prices for the various bullion and coin items turn out to be somewhat higher than their rivals too.

As a place to learn about precious metals, Monex is among the best. You ought to look through their videos and educate yourself on their site. Then you can decide if you want to make them your silver and gold dealer.

GoldSilver.com

Mike Maloney is the iconic purveyor of the coin dealer site GoldSilver.com. With this outfit, he offers you not only the sale and purchase of precious metals, but also third party storage and physical delivery of your bullion. Mr. Maloney is a well known and respected educator as well as investor in gold and silver. He has been Robert Kiyosaki's official Rich Dad Adviser for precious metals since 2005.

The education that Maloney offers you begins with the book that he researched and published, the "Guide to Investing in Gold and Silver." This is still the number one selling precious metals investment book ever. Mike's advice is practical and simple for a novice, as he is originally a self taught precious metals investor.

This makes his website and book both easy to understand, since they are not cluttered with difficult financial terms.

The downsides to GoldSilver.com mostly revolve around size and scale. This is not among the largest of the various gold and silver dealers. While they have a good selection of metals on offer, it is by no means exhaustive.

The site gains many of its points from the goal of Mike Maloney to education you about gold and silver. He not only guides you in what precious metals are doing now, but also in their cyclical movements. The investor education offered by GoldSilver.com invites you to investigate the site as you consider where to purchase your own gold and silver.

Bullion Direct

Bullion Direct is an interesting precious metals site. Besides their standard catalog of gold and silver coins and bullion that they offer online, they have something unique called the Nucleo Exchange. This real time, around the clock, automated exchange is a place where you can sell and buy gold and silver coins with thousands of other interested members for much better prices than from any dealer.

The order matching system pairs bid and ask prices that allow you to lock in your price on the coin that you wish to buy or sell. Bullion Direct takes care of the insurance, storage, distribution, authenticating, and trading of all of these products. This exchange lets you save the dealer profit spreads on gold coins that can mean an extra fifty to one hundred dollars per unit in your pocket.

There are pros and cons to Bullion Direct's other services. They will help you set up a self directed IRA that allows you to put tax deferred retirement money into silver and gold bullion and coins. You own the precious metals but do not keep them physically, as they are stored either in their vaults or those of a third party company.

Their prices on silver and gold coins are not as competitive as with some of the other major dealers. While their inventory is extensive, their website is not as easy to use as Monex. If you do not participate in their nucleo exchange, you may find that some other dealers are more competitive.

Goldline

Goldline boasts fifty full years of experience of selling gold and silver to investors. They number many high profile individuals among their clients, such as Glenn Beck of Fox News. Besides the sale of bullion precious metals, they also offer an extensive range of collectible and rare silver and gold coins.

Goldline has a lot to brag about. Their inventory and website are impressive. The customer service and shipping are both among the best in the industry. The company also offers the convenience of a precious metals IRA.

You can find fault with the fact that Goldline's prices are not spelled out on the website. While Bullion Direct or Apmex specify clearly what they charge, Goldline's prices are suspiciously absent, replaced instead by a "call to order" label. The truth is that their prices are not bad, but this disguised price feature is a turn off to many people who like transparency.

All this is to say that you should call and obtain some prices before you decide to buy from Goldline.

Apmex

Apmex.com is a popular place to purchase gold, silver, platinum, palladium, and collectible bullion and coins. This leading dealer of precious metals' full name is the American Precious Metals Exchange. They live up to their reputation by offering not only an extensive line of precious metal bullion and collector coins, but also precious metals IRA's.

The pros to Apmex lie in their fantastic prices. These are among the lowest in the business. Besides this, they also feature regular discounted items and sales. The products are well packaged so that they arrive to you in good condition, and they ship out in a week or less most of the time.

The only downside to Apmex may be that their website is a little cluttered and complicated to use. For example, you can not quickly or easily find out how long that they have been in business or what dollar value of metals they have exchanged with clients over the years. Other than this, the company features solid customer service, fantastic shipping, frequent discounts, and a terrific price.

VectorVest Stock Analysis And Trading System Review

When you are trying to make money in the stock market, you should first realize that the market is a very complicated and sometimes wild animal.

Look at the way that it has swung up and down by even five hundred points in a single day over the last month since Standard & Poor's downgraded the U.S. government credit rating.

What you need to help you effectively invest in the stock market is a reliable system. VectorVest is one such system that you should seriously consider in your stock market investment efforts.

Who is VectorVest System Creator Dr. Bart DiLiddo?

The creator of the VectorVest system is Dr. Bart DiLiddo. Dr. DiLiddo happens to be among the leading experts on investment in the world. His system has a consistent track record of outperforming market analyst and expert picks.

DiLiddo does not have a background as a stock market guru, analyst, or soothsayer. Instead, he brings to the table the background of well trained mathematician. With a unique perspective that he gained from his time at Fortune 500 companies, he not only understands math, but also business.

Over a thirty year time frame, Dr. DiLiddo has combined his expertise in math along with his invaluable business experience in order to analyze stock performances on an individual stock level. He quantifies their specific risk.

He also looks for and picks out bottoms and tops of various markets with an uncanny degree of accuracy. DiLiddo claims thousands of investors around the globe among his followers. The VectorVest system earns them double and even triple digit returns most years, in either good or bad markets.

Dr. DiLiddo has won the well known "Dart Board" stock picking competition that "The Wall Street Journal" runs. He has written pieces for "Investor Alliances" magazine. Besides this, he also speaks routinely at the Money Show, the American Association of Individual Investors gatherings, and various other financial forums and conferences for investors.

What Exactly is VectorVest?

VectorVest is the system that Dr. DiLiddo actually designed beginning back in 1978. At the time, the brilliant man started to come up with mathematical formulas that succinctly and precisely explain what circumstances lead a stock price to go up or down. In the course of his investigations, he learned that every factor that influences a stock price can actually be described with these mathematically based timing models, value models, and safety models.

DiLiddo tested and re-tested all of his formulas and models before he was satisfied that they worked as planned. The results have been impressive, as his system has helped he and his adherents to make significant profits from the markets not only in good times, but also in times of terrible chaos in the markets.

VectorVest is the tool that can radically improve your stock market investment performance.

It will eliminate the hours of research and educated guesswork that you typically have to employ in order to discover which stocks are the right ones for your portfolio and objectives. This is because the system takes more than 18,300 different stocks each day and graphs, analyzes, and then ranks them according to variables of timing, safety, and value.

The system stands apart from rival systems as the only one that uses both technical and fundamental analysis in the recommendations that it makes. The result is that you can clearly know if you should sell, buy, or hold a stock. This helps you to invest with greater confidence so that you can aim for greater profits while limiting your risk.

One of the best facets of VectorVest is that the system is designed so that any level of investor can make it work. You will not find it complicated at all. All that you have to do is to click through a few screens and choices in order to gain access to incredibly detailed and useful information that will guide you in your investment decisions.

How Does VectorVest Determine Which Stocks You Should Trade?

VectorVest comes up with two different ways to describe appropriate value of an individual stock each day. A stock's main value is determined to show you the present worth of the stock. The system takes into consideration earnings, cash flows, profitability, growth of earnings, interest rates, and inflation levels in this number.

Relative value is also computed based on anticipated price appreciation over three years, the risk measurement of the stock, and the rates of AAA Corporate Bonds. This tells you whether a stock is over valued or under valued.

What Different Products Does the VectorVest Website Offer You?

Vector Vest 7 Real Time

In the U.S., VectorVest Real Time is the most state of the art program that the company and website offers you. This real time platform provides you with literal moment charts and stock analysis. It works through 8,300 different individual stocks and applies forty-one varying parameters, of which twenty-eight are constantly reflected through real time information.

This platform offers you up to the moment buy, sell, or hold suggestions for each of the stocks. The updates for timing the markets are issued in real time as well. This version of VectorVest costs $129 per month, or a reduced price of $1,295 each year.

Vector Vest 7 IntraDay

The next product in the company's line up is the Vector Vest 7 Intraday. This version similarly screens, sorts, ranks, and also graphs the 8,300 stocks with thirty-nine parameters. Twenty-six of these factors are updated with a fifteen minute delay. You still receive the buy, sell, or hold calls each day, as well as the current market timing updates that help you to know what to do throughout the market day. The IntraDay platform costs you $59 per month, or a reduced price of $645 each year.

Vector Vest Mobile

If you are a stock market trader who is away from your computer or laptop all the time, then VectorVest Mobile is the appropriate version of the VectorVest program for you. The tools that it provides are still updated every minute. This gives you instantaneous signals to buy, hold, or sell individual stocks, as with the Real Time version.

Vector Vest 6

For investors who reside outside of the United States, VectorVest offers the VectorVest 6 platform. This is available in a number of countries and areas around the globe. Canada, the United Kingdom, Europe, South Africa, Australia, and Hong Kong residents all have access to this version of the platform.

What Services Does VectorVest Offer You?

Vectorvest.com offers a number of additional services to you. They provide upcoming training seminars in U.S. cities including Chicago, Boston, Dallas, Las Vegas, Seattle, Philadelphia, Phoenix, and Savanna. Besides this, they offer their quality training in Canadian cities like Toronto, Vancouver, St. John's, and Fredericton. In Europe, they do these seminars in such famous cities as Brussels, Amsterdam, Geneva, Frankfurt, Hamburg, and Berlin. In Asia and Africa, these seminars will occur in Australia, Hong Kong, Singapore, and South Africa.

VectorVest Free Stock Analysis

VectorVest will also analyze the stocks in your portfolio for you. They do this for free, as a marketing effort to convince you to try out their system. They will give you as many as three individual stock analyses a day, for a combined total of nine reviews maximum.

VectorVest Research Articles

VectorVest also provides research articles to its subscribers. They promote stocks that are undervalued and safe. They feature stocks that they believe will rise in price.

What is the Free Trial Offer on VectorVest?

Vector Vest offers a completely risk free $9.95 Trial for 5 weeks. This offer includes an instructional CD that is quick and simple to master. You also receive Dr. Bart DiLiddo's "Stocks Strategies, & Common Sense" book.

Finally, you get four free reports on market timing, bottom fishing, options, and shorting stocks. VectorVest values this package at $130. If you do not like the package and program at the end of the five weeks, then you do not have to pay anything else.

Can you find a competing system that offers you so much for such a reasonable amount of money?

Tools

<u>WEALTH</u>

"Pursuing Prosperity with Financial Education"

Wealth

Eight Facts How Entrepreneurs Create Wealth

You will find that you are in good company if you do not fully understand the specifics of wealth. In fact, most people harbor a number of misconceptions about what wealth is and how you should create it.

Wealth is not a magic number of dollars that you accumulate and then retire. In fact, it will surprise you to learn how people who effectively create wealth feel about the money and the process that they use to obtain it.

In the following paragraphs, you will find eight different truths that are worth understanding about wealth.

#1 - Entrepreneurs Create Wealth

Entrepreneurs are the individuals who generate the overwhelming amount of wealth today. People who are entrepreneurs are those who take on the financial risks to start up a new venture. They have an idea or an enterprise, and they are responsible for both the outcome and risks of their idea, service, or product. If you are such an individual, then you are commonly motivated by the innate desire to build up something new and tangible. You have to be willing to make decisions and take risks along the way.

On the list of wealthy people in the world, entrepreneurs take up most of the positions. You will not find many individuals there who call themselves employees. This is because employees work to make money for the owners of their companies, the entrepreneurs.

#2 - The Eight Types of Entrepreneurs

It may surprise you to learn that there are not hundreds of different kinds of entrepreneurs. There is also not a single type of this individual who takes risks. Instead, there are only eight different kinds of entrepreneurs in the world. These are creators, mechanics, stars, supporters, deal makers, traders, accumulators, and lords. Creators are those who come up with the ideas that make profitable businesses. They are not good at daily operations of a business.

Mechanics perfect products and ideas that someone else has already started. Stars are entrepreneurs with strong personalities who enjoy the pressure of delivering results, like CEO's. Supporters are the types who work well with a creator, mechanic, or a star to build up a tremendous business. Deal makers are you who count on your relationships and connections to capture opportunities.

Traders love bargains and put together low buyers with high sellers. If you are an accumulator, then you are a patient person who builds up assets and ideas over time. Finally, lords insist on control of all aspects of an asset and avoid the spot light as they build up wealth. These eight entrepreneur types make up the Wealth Dynamics square.

#3 - Entrepreneurs Have Both Strengths and Weaknesses

You may be surprised that every kind of entrepreneur possesses not only strengths, but also weaknesses, that differentiate them from the other kinds of entrepreneurs. Extroverts will prefer to work with other people instead of processes or information. On the other hand, introverts find their comfort level not with individuals, but with information and processes.

This is why a supporter and a deal maker are so effective at inter-facing with other people. It also helps to explain why creators, mechanics, and lords would rather work with their ideas and assets more than manage and interact with individuals. This does not make one type of entrepreneur superior or inferior. It only highlights their differences from the other kinds.

#4 - Some Wealth Strategies Match With Entrepreneurs Better Than Others

Your different strengths and weaknesses cause you to be more effective at particular strategies for building up wealth and less effective at other strategies. Take a Star kind of entrepreneur as an example. They excel in situations where their creativity is called upon to communicate a brand. They would not do so well at the creation of an idea or a brand though. A mechanic would get best results in work to perfect a process like a franchise. If you ask a mechanic to come up with the idea from scratch, the individual will be out of his or her comfort zone.

#5 - The Proper Focus on How to Create Wealth

Once you know which type of entrepreneur you are, you will gain the ability to know where you should concentrate your efforts.

This will tell you what strategy is the best one for you to apply yourself towards wealth creation.

The sad part is that if you do not clearly understand what your entrepreneur type is, then you will probably work on strategies that do not fit you well. This can lead to disappointment when you fail or only achieve a small amount of success at your particular endeavor. If you trade stocks when you are most suited to run a franchise, then you will find that you do not get the proper satisfaction or success from this activity.

#6 - Work with Individuals Who Compliment You

No one is truly a self made millionaire. Major wealth is built up when you employ a group of people who are good at their tasks. Once you know your own strengths and weaknesses, then you will understand the right type of people that you need to find and engage.

The key is to find the best people and give them tasks that will fully utilize their own best talents and abilities. This way, you will be able to put efficient teams in to place and to magnify your own efforts. You will find that your creative talents will work with much better effects when you have terrific teams who stand behind you.

#7 - Applying The Wrong Strategy Feels Like Difficult Work

If you work at an enterprise that feels like hard work, then something is wrong. Wealth creation should not feel like such difficult work. When you follow the strategy that is the proper one for you, then it will feel completely different. For example, if you enjoy public speaking, then you will thrive at it.

Someone else might learn to do it and even become good at it, but if this person does not enjoy it, it will still feel like work. When you find your best strategy, you will actually enjoy the work.

#8 - When You Build Up Wealth Properly, It Will Feel Satisfying

This is a point that far too many people fail to realize. If you build wealth with your best personal strategy, and use the talents of people who complement your weaknesses, then you will find an immense satisfaction when you work to build up wealth.

Consider some of the richest individuals in the world. If you study them, you will discover that only a few of them have chosen to retire early. Instead, they continue to work so long as their body will let them. The truth is that if it was such a burden to build up great wealth, then most of them would have stopped as soon as they made their first fortune.

Would you continue to labor at something that you did not enjoy immensely if you were already financially secure?

The Ten Truths of Financial Wealth Creation Revealed

Have you ever wondered why the financial adviser industry is still promoting the same old tired "buy and hold" long term strategy that it was promoting to your parents and grandparents? The author of a new book entitled "The Ten Truths of Wealth Creation," John E. Girouard, says that while the spirit of vision and change in industry, medicine, fine arts, and the military is encouraged and rewarded, in the investment business it is heavily frowned upon.

Not only this, but the investment advisory business depends on the lack of change and on the confusion of you the investor in order to thrive. In the paragraphs that follow, you will understand why "The Ten Truths of Wealth Creation" is a must read book that can save your failing prospects of retirement and financial security, regardless of where you are now.

About the Author John E. Girouard

John Girouard is the CEO and President of Washington D.C. based Capital Asset Management Group. He has now occupied this position since 1984. He also created the Institute for Financial Independence that provides education and resources to businesses and people on planning, long range financial goals, and investment strategies.

He routinely speaks at both association and industry meetings. He teaches classes at various financial centers of learning in Delaware and Maryland. Girouard is the recipient of numerous certifications and awards within his industry. He obtained his Bachelor of Arts in Economics at the University of Maryland at College Park.

Opportunities Your Financial Adviser Will Never Discuss With You

Girouard's "Ten Truths of Wealth Creation" book is a no non-sense, basics investment guide that shows how the trusted financial advisers in the business hand out poor advice to you and peddle you terribly constructed investment packages. The goal of these charlatans is to enrich themselves and the companies for which they work, all at your personal expense.

You should understand that this is not a get rich quick or slow product. Instead, it is an eye opening examination of the many missteps that you and others fall victim to in your own personal long term finances. It offers solutions to free up the inherent money-increasing opportunities that you never hear your financial adviser discuss.

You may not know that your income is actually taxed several different times. Yet you can make choices with your money and investments that legally reduce the number of times that your money is taxed. These dollars that you save can turn out to be an enormous amount of money that you can instead put to work on your own behalf in the practice of earning more wealth.

This book and author demonstrate to you some time tested and proven ideas that will enable you to achieve these goals in your own personal life. When you follow his advice, you can do this with both safety and expediency, whether the market is negative, positive, or indecisive.

What Are The Ten Truths of Wealth Creation?

The book features chapters divided up into several sections that focus on the ten truths of wealth creation. John Girouard came up with them throughout his twenty-five year career as an investment adviser professional.

He made it a point to challenge his bosses and the establishment early on, since he refused to sell junk products to his clients. You should listen to these truths carefully. They may save your retirement and even entire financial future. These are the ten key truths for you to create wealth in your own life and personal finances.

Truth No. 1 "The Key to Wealth is Through Ownership and Control, not Financial Products."

You will almost never build your fortune with tricky and exotic financial products. It is when you buy, control, and own hard assets such as property and life insurance products that you will build up your wealth. Part ways with your expensive financial adviser and his firm right away.

Truth No. 2. "The More Money Moves, the More Wealth is Created."

When your money is moving from one holding to another it grows in value. This is true with whole life insurance. You can borrow your own money from this and use it to invest interest free in other products, even as it gains interest and dividends as if it were still sitting in the policy.

Truth No. 3. "Everything in Life Has A Cost and Requires Payments."

The old adage that there is no free lunch rings true for your finances. You will have to save money and put it somewhere to build up assets and wealth. This will cost you money that you put aside on a regular basis.

Truth No. 4. "The Biggest cost to Wealth- Up to Sixty Percent - Is Uncaptured Interest Income, Unnecessary Interest Expense, and Failure to Manage Taxes."

The greatest expense when you purchase anything is on interest that you pay. You can borrow from yourself and become your own bank using a whole life insurance policy. When you pay too much in taxes, you are only cheating your own financial future.

Truth No. 5. "Rates of Return and Index Investing as Financial Planning Tools are Misleading and Meaningless."

Do not believe the garbage that Wall Street publishes and pushes on you.

There are no real rates of return in the stock market at a consistent ten percent over decades. When you factor in compound interest, whole life insurance policies and dividends that pay five to six percent are superior, sustainable, and bankable.

Truth No. 6. "Insurance is a Contract, and Understanding this Concept is the Key to Creating and Preserving Wealth."

You must understand what you get into with your insurance contract. When you build the right type of whole life policy, you will get far ahead. This will include dividend payment and riders that guarantee at least a portion of your money is invested for greater guaranteed rates of return.

Truth No. 7. "Risk is Not About Losing Money."

Risk is not really about the possibility to lose money. It is more about the lost opportunity to make too small a return to secure your financial future and retirement. You must avoid this real risk at all costs. Risky is when you drive your car without any driving experience and without insurance. Risk is when you have insurance on your car and practice in driving your car. You are aware of the risk and you can manage it.

Truth No. 8. "Some Debt is Good, If You Finance a Thing No Longer than its Useful Life."

Bad debt is debt you acquire to buy things with no useful productive capacity.

Good debt creates cash flow and income from investments. You should never finance something for longer than it generates income or usefulness.

Truth No. 9. "The Biggest Obstacle to Building Wealth is the Absence of Reliable Market Information."

The Wall Street firms have almost exclusive access to the best market information. You will have to find a source of this too. Good financial education will help you in this endeavor.

Truth No. 10: "Financial Independence Begins with Understanding and Focusing on Your Life's Goals As Opposed to Financial Goals, and Minimizing Your Future Decisions."

You will not achieve financial independence until you realize what the goals for your life are. You must try to reduce the amount of decisions that you have to wrestle with in the future. Additional numbers of choices lead to greater risks that you might make a mistake or even a series of mistakes.

Verdict of the Ten Truths of Wealth Creation Book

Reviewers of this book have sadly stated that had millions of Americans been aware of this book's advice and truths but a few years ago, they might have saved the loss of literally hundreds of thousands of dollars each. While it is too late to save money that has already been lost, it is never too late to start salvaging the future.

Now more than ever, you and other readers need a way to make every dollar go further for your future and retirement prospects to be secured. If you do not do something soon, then you will still have the same pitiful results to look forward to in five and ten years from now. Doing nothing is also a choice, though it may be a poor one at that.

You have nothing to lose in picking up a copy of this book. At the same time, there is everything to gain when you learn about the ten truths of wealth creation. What is stopping you from increasing your financial education today?

The Most Effective Ways to Build Up Wealth in Your Life

If you are like the majority of people, then you do not have a large trust fund that waits for you or a big cash settlement from a lawsuit to help you meet your financial goals and to retire. For you to obtain wealth, you will have to achieve it on your own.

This is what is meant by the phrase to pull yourself up by your bootstraps. But while you probably agree with this assessment of your own financial prospects, you likely do not know how it is that you can grow wealthy.

There are some financial secrets that may seem somewhat obvious once you hear them. Pay attention to these so that you can learn the most effective ways to build up wealth in your own life.

Wealth is Usually Built Up Slowly

This may be frustrating to hear, but wealth is not usually built up quickly. Instead, it is achieved when you carefully and deliberately make a plan, adjust it as circumstances dictate, and then work hard to follow through with it. You are only deluding yourself if you think that you will suddenly achieve wealth in a lottery like fashion.

The first secret that you have to internalize is that you will probably spend many years in the quest to build up wealth and become wealthy. It may even take you until you approach retirement age. The important thing is that you are on the right path and that you take steps to reach your goal every day. Until you start the journey towards this destination, you will certainly not arrive there.

Wealth is Achieved Through A Simple Formula

For the vast majority of people like you, wealth is reached when you follow a simple and not too flashy formula. This is that wealth equals savings plus investment. In other words, there are two components that you must work on in your quest to achieve wealth.

Saving is a time honored concept that has mostly become a lost art in the United States in the past few decades. Until the Great Recession and Financial Crisis changed everything about people's attitudes towards savings, the personal savings rate in the U.S. stood at from about zero to negative numbers.

It has increased to more than five percent in the wake of the failures of banks, major unemployment, and credit line reductions that you have seen close to you or personally experienced. Still, the savings rate in this country is the lowest in the industrial, developed world. Consider that in France and Germany, it is over ten percent.

Financial experts suggest that you should save ten percent of your income.

Retirement planners will tell you that you need to put aside fifteen percent of your earnings if you wish to reach a somewhat reasonable level of replacing half of your working income when you arrive at the age to retire or at least to work less hours. If you want to achieve real wealth, you may need to save even more than this amount.

You Must Begin to Invest In Order to Achieve Real Wealth

The second part of the equation is perhaps the most important one. While you must save money in order to have money to invest, you will most likely never get ahead if you simply sock away your money in your mattress or in a low interest account that serves to barely keep your money ahead of the annual rate of inflation.

Instead, you have to look for investments opportunities that can appreciably grow your money. There are many of them out there, but some of them are better than others. To learn which ones are the most appropriate places for your money, you should begin to educate yourself financially.

All of the Wealthy Build Up a Financial Education

One thing that the rich practically all have in common is that they take the time to learn about how to grow their money. The school system certainly does not teach this. There are many ways to educate yourself financially.

You can take some classes on finance and investment at your local community college or university. This will take some time and money, but it is a wise way to spend both. You can also educate yourself through reading good books for personal finance and investing.

A good one to start with is Robert Kiyosaki's "Rich Dad, Poor Dad" series. This is an excellent entry level book that will start to give you some background on and comprehension of sensible techniques in investing.

If you read one financial or investing book a month, you would be amazed at how much you would know and understand about money management and investing at the end of the year. Newspaper and magazine articles will help to keep you on the cutting edge of what is happening with the investment world.

You can also attend seminars and workshops on investing your money wisely. There are many of these that guest speakers offer around the country. There will be some cost involved, but you can learn a lot in only a single day or two through such events. You should never stop learning about and listening to ways to manage your money.

The Rich Put Money To Work For Them

The saying that the rich do not work for money, they make money work for them is very true. They do this through a concept called passive income. Passive income is a means of generating money that you do not directly work for with your time and skills. It involves building up some form or stream of income that will continue to provide you with regular and periodic cash flow. Cash flow investments like these are critical if you are going to build up sustainable wealth.

There are countless examples of passive income and cash flow investments that you can pursue. The most popular one these days is to establish an Internet based business.

This might involve you starting up a blog and gathering up advertisers to bring in money. You might also create some form or e-commerce store to sell products, information, or ideas. Passive income and cash flow investments like these can take some time to build up, but they will provide you with an additional stream of revenue that you need to achieve wealth more rapidly.

Many kinds of investments are also considered passive income or cash flow types. If you buy a rental property house and rent it out, the income that this produces is passive and yields helpful cash flow. You can also put your money into mutual funds, investment funds, and stocks that pay high dividends. These will provide you with monthly or quarterly checks that help to supplement your income and aid you on your way to growing wealthy.

The Rich Know Where the Back Door Is Located

This last point may amuse you, but it is so true. One thing that separates the wealthy from you and the rest of Americans is that they always know where they back door is in any establishment that they find themselves. This is to say that they always have a back up or alternate plan ready in case their first one does not work out. Have you considered where the back door is in your own financial situation and plan lately?

Wealth

<u>RESOURCES</u>

"Free Bonus Content"

Resources

For additional 'Wealth Advisor' editions please check our website or go to amazon.com.

Get All 'Wealth Advisor' Editions
www.wealthbuildingcourse.com/wealth-advisor

At present we are offering a free membership to the Wealth Building Course. This membership is free as long the full course is in development. The current release date will we in 2012 and the course will be priced at $799.

Sign Up For Your Free Wealth Education Membership:
www.wealthbuildingcourse.com

If you have additional interest in preserving your wealth and invest in silver please check out the author's book: 'Building Wealth with Silver', which is available at amazon.

Building Wealth with Silver Book:
www.wealthbuildingcourse.com/silver-book

The author also developed a very sophisticated course around silver investment, which is available for purchase online. The 'Silver Fortune Formula' course reveals every detail for successful silver investing.

Silver Investment 101:
www.wealthbuildingcourse.com/silver

Resources

Thomas Herold, CEO – Co-founder Wealth Building Course

Thomas Herold is a successful entrepreneur and personal development coach. After a career with one of the largest electronic companies in the world, he realized that a regular job would never fully satisfy his need for connection on a deep level.

The only way to live his full potential was to start building his own business and find new ways to be in service to others.

For over 25 years he has helped many people – including himself – build their dream businesses. Toward that goal, he focuses on education – simplified and enhanced by modern technology. He is the author of three books with over 200,000 copies distributed worldwide.

Other than his passion for creating businesses, Thomas has spent over 20 years in the self-development field. Placing emphasis on the exploration of consciousness and building practical applications that allow people to express their purpose and passion in life, Thomas's work in this area has provided ample and happy proof that this approach works.

He believes that every person has at least one gift and that, when this gift is developed and nourished, it will serve as a fountainhead of personal happiness and help contribute to a better, more sustainable world.

For the past three years Thomas Herold has studied the monetary system and has experienced some profound insights on how money and wealth are related. He has recently committed to sharing this knowledge in a new venture – the Wealth Building Course, a website along with educational materials that designed to help people get started on their own money makeover and get a financial education in the process.

Thomas's ultimate vision for the Wealth Building Course is to empower people to adopt a wealthy mindset and to create abundance for themselves and others. His ability to explain complex information in simple terms makes him an outstanding teacher and coach.

www.ingramcontent.com/pod-product-compliance
Lightning Source LLC
Chambersburg PA
CBHW051446170526
45166CB00001B/138